HOLY SMOKES

HOLY SMOKES

FAITH, FELLOWSHIP, AND FIRE

A GUIDE FOR MEN WHO GATHER
OVER CIGARS, COFFEE, AND SCRIPTURE

BRIAN L. VIERS

VIA Press
Chicago / Nashville / Tampa
2025

This Holy Smokes mission and guidebook is dedicated to supportive, faithful, and understanding spouses who have encouraged us to become better men.

Copyright © Brian L. Viers 2025

Under copyright above, no part of this publication may be used or reproduced in print or shared on internet without written permission by the author (owner of copyright) and publisher (VIA Press).

Book Layout by Sharon Viers

All Scripture quotations, unless otherwise indicated, are taken from the Holy Bible, New International Version®, NIV®. Copyright ©1973, 1978, 1984, 2011 by Biblica, Inc.™ Used by permission of Zondervan. All rights reserved worldwide. www.zondervan.com. The "NIV" and "New International Version" are trademarks registered in the United States Patent and Trademark Office by Biblica, Inc.™

ISBN# 978-0-9996072-6-8

Printed in the USA

This Holy Smokes mission and guidebook is dedicated to supportive, faithful, and understanding spouses who have encouraged us to become better men.

Copyright © Brian L. Viers 2025

Under copyright above, no part of this publication may be used or reproduced in print or shared on internet without written permission by the author (owner of copyright) and publisher (VIA Press).

Book Layout by Sharon Viers

All Scripture quotations, unless otherwise indicated, are taken from the Holy Bible, New International Version®, NIV®. Copyright ©1973, 1978, 1984, 2011 by Biblica, Inc.™ Used by permission of Zondervan. All rights reserved worldwide. www.zondervan.com. The "NIV" and "New International Version" are trademarks registered in the United States Patent and Trademark Office by Biblica, Inc.™

ISBN# 978-0-9996072-6-8

Printed in the USA

TABLE OF CONTENTS

Introduction 5

January...8

February..40

March..69

April..101

May..132

June...165

July..196

August...228

September..260

October..291

November...323

December...354

Introduction

Strength in Brotherhood

In today's fast-paced, ever-changing world, men often feel the weight of responsibilities—providing for their families, striving for success, maintaining relationships, and navigating the challenges of faith. Yet too often, these burdens are carried alone. We live in a culture that sometimes equates masculinity with isolation and silent struggle, leaving little room for openness, vulnerability, or authentic connection. This isn't where your identity was intended to align.

But God never intended for us to walk this journey alone. From the very beginning, He designed us for community, for relationships that sharpen us, encourage us, and hold us accountable. Proverbs 27:17 reminds us, "As iron sharpens iron, so one man sharpens another." True strength is found not in isolation, but in brotherhood—in coming together with like-minded men who are committed to growing in faith, standing firm against temptation, and pursuing the life God has called them to live.

This devotional is an invitation to experience that brotherhood. It's not just about studying scripture and deepening your relationship with God (though that is foundational); it's also about building meaningful connections with other men. It's about creating a safe space where you can be honest about your struggles, your doubts, and your victories—without judgment. It's about holding each other accountable, encouraging one another to stay the course, and celebrating the victories that come from walking in obedience to God's Word.

Men's cigar and coffee gatherings are the perfect setting for this. There's something profound and gratifying about sitting shoulder-to-shoulder, sharing in conversation over the simple pleasures of a fine cigar and a good cup of coffee. However, don't think you need to be, or we are suggesting you inherit either habit but instead, show up as you are. The Bible tells us to come as we are and to make disciples of all nations. These gatherings merely offer an opportunity to strip away the distractions of life and focus on what matters most—your relationship with God, your growth as a man of faith, and your role as a leader in your home, church, and community.

Each day in this devotional is designed to speak to the unique challenges men face. Topics like temptation, identity, leadership, family, work, and purpose are explored through the lens of scripture, offering practical wisdom for living a life of obedience. Most importantly, each devotional calls you to action, urging you to apply what you've learned in your own life and to lean on your brothers for encouragement and support—living a life of significance.

The goal isn't perfection—it's progress. Together, as brothers in Christ, we can confront the areas where we fall short, grow stronger in our faith, and encourage one another to live as the men God has called us to be.

So, join us on this 365-day journey. Come with an open heart, a willingness to grow, and a commitment to being honest—with yourself, with your brothers, and with God. Let's walk this road together, holding one another accountable, lifting each other up, and discovering the strength that comes from living in the light of God's truth.

It's time to rise together. Iron sharpens iron. Let's get started!

January

Foundations for Godly Living

It's all about beginnings.

This month we will explore the crucial steps to building and maintaining a strong foundation.

January 1

Built to Last: Establishing a Strong Foundation

"Therefore everyone who hears these words of mine and puts them into practice is like a wise man who built his house on the rock. The rain came down, the streams rose, and the winds blew and beat against that house; yet it did not fall, because it had its foundation on the rock." (Matthew 7:24-25, NIV)

True strength in life comes from trusting God's Word. When we live by His teachings, we build a solid foundation that can handle any challenge. This passage reminds us to not just listen to God, but to act on His Word, so our lives are firmly rooted in His unshakable power.

The Last Ash: How can you make God's Word the cornerstone of your decisions today?

The Final Sip: Does your foundation need reinforcement through prayer and Scripture?

January 2

The Strength to Lead: A Call to Biblical Manhood

"Be on your guard; stand firm in the faith; be courageous; be strong. Do everything in love." (1 Corinthians 16:13-14, NIV)

True strength in leadership comes from standing firm in faith, being courageous, and showing love. This passage calls men to lead with integrity and strength, not through dominance, but by living out God's commands with boldness and compassion. It encourages men lead others with love, reflecting the heart of biblical manhood.

The Last Ash: What does being watchful and standing firm in faith look like in your daily life?

The Final Sip: How can you grow in love while showing strength as a biblical leader?

January 3

When Pressure Mounts: Standing Firm in the Faith

"Be alert and of sober mind. Your enemy the devil prowls around like a roaring lion looking for someone to devour. Resist him, standing firm in the faith, because you know that the family of believers throughout the world is undergoing the same kind of sufferings." (1 Peter 5:8-9, NIV)

True strength in the face of pressure comes from resisting the enemy with a firm faith. This passage encourages believers to remain faithful, knowing that others face similar trials. God's promises, especially when we feel overwhelmed, reminding us that strength comes not from our own abilities, but from our unwavering trust in God's faithfulness.

The Last Ash: What practical steps can you take to resist the enemy when challenges arise?

The Final Sip: How has standing firm in faith strengthened your relationship with God?

January 4

A Man After God's Heart: Lessons from David

"After removing Saul, he made David their king. God testified concerning him: 'I have found David son of Jesse, a man after my own heart; he will do everything I want him to do.'"
(Acts 13:22, NIV)

True devotion to God comes from a heart that desires to follow His will above all else. David's life teaches us that pursuing God's heart means consistently seeking His direction, even when we fall short. This passage encourages us to examine our own hearts and focus on aligning our lives with God's purposes. It's a call to cultivate a heart that is responsive to God's leading, seeking to honor Him in every area of life.

The Last Ash: How can you cultivate a heart that seeks God above all else?

The Final Sip: What areas of your life need better alignment with God's purposes?

January 5

Integrity in the Small Details

"Whoever can be trusted with very little can also be trusted with much, and whoever is dishonest with very little will also be dishonest with much." (Luke 16:10, NIV)

Integrity is formed by our faithfulness in everyday actions, no matter how small they may seem. This passage reminds us that being trustworthy in little things prepares us for greater responsibilities in God's Kingdom. It encourages us to cultivate honesty, dependability, and faithfulness in all areas of life, knowing that God values our integrity in the small matters just as much as the big ones. Through this, we reflect God's character and grow in trustworthiness and leadership.

The Last Ash: How can small acts of faithfulness today prepare you for greater responsibilities?

The Final Sip: In what ways does living with integrity reflect God's character to others?

January 6

The Power of Accountability

"Two are better than one, because they have a good return for their labor: If either of them falls down, one can help the other up. But pity anyone who falls and has no one to help them up." (Ecclesiastes 4:9-10, NIV)

True strength comes from standing together with others who share our values and faith. This scripture reminds us that accountability is not just about sharing burdens but also about helping each other grow and succeed. When we stand together we can overcome challenges more easily ensuring that we stay on the right path and continue to grow in character and faith.

The Last Ash: Who is walking alongside you as a source of strength and encouragement?

The Final Sip: How can you be a better accountability partner to a brother in Christ?

January 7

Guarding Your Eyes, Guarding Your Heart

"Above all else, guard your heart, for everything you do flows from it." (Proverbs 4:23, NIV)

True wisdom involves being intentional about what we allow into our hearts and minds. This verse reminds us that our thoughts and desires shape our actions, so we must be cautious about what we see, hear, and allow to influence us. Guarding our eyes and hearts means actively choosing to focus on things that uplift and strengthen us, steering clear of distractions or temptations that might lead us astray. By doing so, we protect and align ourselves more closely with God's will.

The Last Ash: What boundaries do you need to set to protect your heart and mind?

The Final Sip: How can you consistently fix your eyes on what is true and pure?

January 8

Daily Armor: Putting on the Full Armor of God

"Finally, be strong in the Lord and in his mighty power. Put on the full armor of God, so that you can take your stand against the devil's schemes." (Ephesians 6:10-11, NIV)

True strength in spiritual warfare comes from relying on God's power and protection. Paul encourages us to suit up with the armor of God each day, which includes truth, righteousness, peace, faith, salvation, and the Word of God. Each piece serves to protect us from the enemy's lies and temptations. This passage teaches us that our strength isn't found in ourselves but in God's power, and when we arm ourselves with His truth, we can stand firm against all challenges that come our way.

The Last Ash: Which piece of God's armor do you often overlook, and how can you strengthen it?

The Final Sip: How can you make putting on God's armor a daily habit?

January 9

Anchored in Christ During Life's Storms

"We have this hope as an anchor for the soul, firm and secure. It enters the inner sanctuary behind the curtain."
(Hebrews 6:19, NIV)

True security in life comes from being anchored in Christ, especially during times of uncertainty. Just as an anchor keeps a ship steady during rough waters, our hope in Jesus keeps our hearts grounded amid life's storms. This passage encourages us to rely on Christ's faithfulness and His promises, knowing that no matter how fierce the winds of adversity may blow, our souls remain anchored in His unchanging love.

 **The Last Ash:** Be intentional. What anchors you when life feels uncertain or overwhelming?

The Final Sip: How does your hope in Christ provide stability in turbulent times?

January 10

Pride or Humility: Choosing the Better Path

"Humble yourselves before the Lord, and he will lift you up." (James 4:10, NIV)

Humility leads to true greatness in God's eyes, while pride leads to a fall. This passage challenges us to examine our hearts and choose the path of humility, trusting that when we place ourselves under God's authority, He will honor us in a way that far surpasses any self-glorification. It encourages us to rely not on our own strength, but on God's grace and timing.

The Last Ash: In what areas do you need to humble yourself before God today?

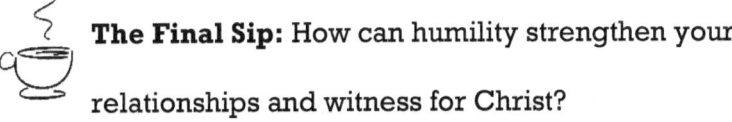

The Final Sip: How can humility strengthen your relationships and witness for Christ?

January 11

Being a Light in the Workplace

"In the same way, let your light shine before others, that they may see your good deeds and glorify your Father in heaven." (Matthew 5:16, NIV)

As followers of Christ, we are called to be a reflection of His light, especially in our profession. This passage challenges us to approach our work with integrity, kindness, and excellence, showing others the difference that a relationship with God makes. When we let our light shine in our daily tasks, our workplace becomes an opportunity to glorify God and influence those around us.

 **The Last Ash:** How can you let your light shine at work today?

The Final Sip: What small but significant acts of kindness can you offer to your coworkers?

January 12

Responding to Life's Challenges with Resilience

"Not only so, but we also glory in our sufferings, because we know that suffering produces perseverance; perseverance, character; and character, hope." (Romans 5:3-4, NIV)

True strength is often forged in the fire of hardship. This passage teaches us that trials are not wasted; they produce perseverance, which builds character and leads to hope. As we face challenges in life, we can trust that God is using them to refine us and strengthen our faith. The process may not be easy, but it leads to a deeper reliance on God and a greater hope in His promises.

The Last Ash: How has a recent challenge helped shape your character?

The Final Sip: In what ways can you embrace challenges as opportunities for growth?

January 13

Equipped for the Battle

"But since we belong to the day, let us be sober, putting on faith and love as a breastplate, and the hope of salvation as a helmet." (1 Thessalonians 5:8, NIV)

The breastplate of faith and love protects our hearts, guarding us from doubt, fear, and selfishness, while the helmet of hope in salvation protects our minds from despair and discouragement. This verse encourages us to stay alert and grounded in Christ, drawing strength from our faith, showing love to others, and holding fast to the hope of eternal life. As men called to lead and influence, we must put on this spiritual armor daily to stand firm and be an example in a world filled with distractions and challenges.

The Last Ash: How can you show faith and love more intentionally in your relationships?

The Final Sip: How can the hope of salvation give you strength and perspective during difficult times?

January 14

Trusting God's Timing

"There is a time for everything, and a season for every activity under the heavens." (Ecclesiastes 3:1, NIV)

True strength is found in trusting that God's timing is perfect. This passage reminds us that everything has a purpose and a season in God's plan. When we trust in His perfect timing, we are free from the pressure of rushing or worrying about the future. Instead, we can rest in the assurance that God's timing is always right and that He is in control of every season of our lives.

The Last Ash: How can you surrender your timing to God's perfect plan today?

The Final Sip: What area of your life do you need to trust God's timing more?

January 15

The Fruit of the Spirit: Living a Life of Strength

"But the fruit of the Spirit is love, joy, peace, forbearance, kindness, goodness, faithfulness, gentleness and self-control. Against such things there is no law." (Galatians 5:22-23, NIV)

True strength is found in the Spirit's work in our lives. This passage speaks of the fruit of the Spirit, qualities that reflect Christ's character and demonstrate His power working within us. As we yield to the Spirit's guidance, we cultivate these virtues, which in turn strengthen our witness to others. It is through the Spirit that we become who God has called us to be, living lives full of love, peace, and self-control.

 **The Last Ash:** Which fruit of the Spirit do you feel God is growing in you right now?

The Final Sip: How can you better cultivate these qualities in your relationships and daily life?

January 16

Taming the Tongue

"The tongue is also a fire, a world of evil among the parts of the body. It corrupts the whole body, sets the whole course of one's life on fire, and is itself set on fire by hell." (James 3:5-6, NIV)

The tongue has immense power to build up or tear down. James warns us about the destructive potential of our words. When we use our speech carelessly or negatively, it can harm relationships, damage reputations, and cause deep emotional pain. But when we control our tongue, it reflects wisdom and maturity in Christ.

 **The Last Ash**: How can you take control of your words today to reflect God's love and wisdom?

The Final Sip: What steps can you take to guard your speech and avoid negative or hurtful words?

January 17

The Importance of Prayer

"Do not be anxious about anything, but in every situation, by prayer and petition, with thanksgiving, present your requests to God." (Philippians 4:6, NIV)

Prayer is a powerful way to seek God's guidance, share our concerns, and express gratitude. Instead of letting anxiety consume us, we are encouraged to turn to God in prayer. Through this act, we not only release our burdens but also receive peace that guards our hearts and minds.

 **The Last Ash**: What specific areas in your life do you need to bring before God in prayer today?

The Final Sip: How can you incorporate more consistent prayer into your routine?

January 18

Living with Integrity

"Whoever walks in integrity walks securely, but whoever takes crooked paths will be found out." (Proverbs 10:9, NIV)

Integrity means doing the right thing even when no one is watching. It's a reflection of our character and our commitment to God's ways. When we live with integrity, we walk confidently, knowing that we are aligned with God's truth. But when we stray from integrity, we risk exposure and loss of trust.

The Last Ash: Are there areas in your life where you need to realign with integrity?

The Final Sip: How does living with integrity give you peace and security?

January 19

God's Faithfulness in Times of Trouble

"Praise be to the God and Father of our Lord Jesus Christ, the Father of compassion and the God of all comfort, who comforts us in all our troubles, so that we can comfort those in any trouble with the comfort we ourselves receive from God." (2 Corinthians 1:3-4, NIV)

God is faithful to comfort us in our struggles and to use our pain to help others. When we face hardships, we can find solace knowing that God's presence is with us. Moreover, the comfort we receive from Him enables us to offer hope and encouragement to others in similar situations.

The Last Ash: How has God comforted you during tough times?

The Final Sip: Who around you might need the comfort that God has given you?

January 20

Trusting God's Timing

"He has made everything beautiful in its time. He has also set eternity in the human heart; yet no one can fathom what God has done from beginning to end." (Ecclesiastes 3:11, NIV)

God has perfect timing, and He orchestrates every detail of our lives. While we often try to rush or control the outcome of situations, God reminds us that everything will unfold in its appointed time. Trusting His timing allows us to rest in His sovereignty and receive the beauty of His plans for us.

The Last Ash: How can you trust God's timing in areas where you are anxious or waiting?

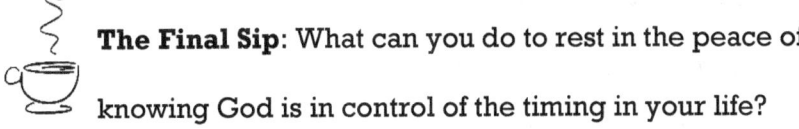

The Final Sip: What can you do to rest in the peace of knowing God is in control of the timing in your life?

January 21

The Power of Encouragement

"And let us consider how we may spur one another on toward love and good deeds, not giving up meeting together, as some are in the habit of doing, but encouraging one another—and all the more as you see the Day approaching."
(Hebrews 10:24-25, NIV)

Encouragement is a powerful tool in building up others in their faith and in their personal lives. We are called to spur each other on toward love and good works, especially as we approach the return of Christ. Encouragement helps people stay focused, motivated, and grounded in the hope we have in Jesus.

The Last Ash: Who can you encourage today to keep pursuing love and good deeds?

The Final Sip: How can you make encouragement a regular part of your interactions with others?

January 22

Seeking God's Wisdom

"If any of you lacks wisdom, let him ask of God, who gives to all liberally and without reproach, and it will be given to him." (James 1:5, NIV)

God is generous with wisdom, offering it freely to those who seek it. When we lack understanding or are facing difficult decisions, we can confidently ask God for guidance. His wisdom leads us to make choices that honor Him and align with His will.

 **The Last Ash**: Are there areas in your life where you need God's wisdom right now?

The Final Sip: How can you ask God for wisdom today and trust in His generous response?

January 23

God's Love and Our Identity

"See what great love the Father has lavished on us, that we should be called children of God! And that is what we are!" (1 John 3:1, NIV)

Understanding God's love for us is foundational to knowing who we are. We are not defined by our past, our failures, or our circumstances; we are defined by the incredible love of God. As His children, we are heirs to His promises and recipients of His grace.

The Last Ash: How does knowing that you are a child of God change the way you view yourself?

The Final Sip: How can you reflect God's love to others in a tangible way today?

January 24

Humility in Serving Others

"Do nothing out of selfish ambition or vain conceit. Rather, in humility value others above yourselves, not looking to your own interests but each of you to the interests of the others." (Philippians 2:3-4, NIV)

Humility is the heart of true service. Jesus modeled this by serving others, even though He was King. We are called to humble ourselves, putting the needs of others first. When we serve with humility, we reflect Christ's love and bring glory to God.

 **The Last Ash**: How can you serve others today with humility and selflessness?

The Final Sip: What's one way you can prioritize the interests of others over your own today?

January 25

The Gift of Grace

"For it is by grace you have been saved, through faith—and this is not from yourselves, it is the gift of God—not by works, so that no one can boast." (Ephesians 2:8-9, NIV)

Grace is God's unmerited favor toward us. It is not something we can earn, but a gift freely given through faith in Jesus Christ. Our salvation is completely by grace, not by our efforts. This truth frees us from striving to be good enough and reminds us to rest in God's love and mercy.

The Last Ash: How can you embrace God's grace today and share it with others?

The Final Sip: How does understanding that salvation is a gift rather than a reward change your perspective?

January 26

Strength in Weakness

"But he said to me, 'My grace is sufficient for you, for my power is made perfect in weakness.' Therefore I will boast all the more gladly of my weaknesses, so that the power of Christ may rest upon me." (2 Corinthians 12:9, NIV)

God's strength is made perfect in our weaknesses. When we acknowledge our limitations and depend on Him, His power is evident in our lives. Rather than seeing weakness as something to hide, we can embrace it as a place where God's grace shines most brightly.

The Last Ash: In what area of your life do you need to lean more fully on God's strength?

The Final Sip: How can you embrace your weakness as a way to experience God's power?

January 27

The Power of Gratitude

"Rejoice always, pray continually, give thanks in all circumstances; for this is God's will for you in Christ Jesus." (1 Thessalonians 5:16-18, NIV)

Gratitude is a powerful expression of faith. Paul encourages believers to maintain an attitude of joy and thankfulness regardless of circumstances. Giving thanks in all things helps us focus on God's goodness and sovereignty, shifting our hearts from complaint to praise.

The Last Ash: How can you cultivate gratitude in your life today, regardless of your circumstances?

The Final Sip: What specific things can you thank God for today, even in tough moments?

January 28

The Blessing of Obedience

"Anyone who loves me will obey my teaching. My Father will love them, and we will come to them and make our home with them. Anyone who does not love me will not obey my teaching. These words you hear are not my own; they belong to the Father who sent me." (John 14:23-24, NIV)

Obedience to God is a sign of our love for Him. Jesus teaches that when we obey His commands, we invite God to dwell within us. This intimate relationship is a result of our willingness to follow His ways, which leads to greater peace, joy, and closeness with God.

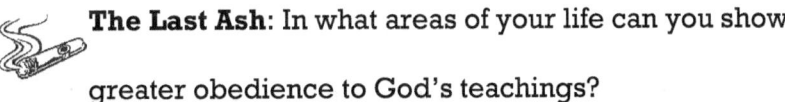**The Last Ash**: In what areas of your life can you show greater obedience to God's teachings?

**The Final Sip**: How does obedience bring you closer to God and experience His love?

January 29

Perseverance in Trials

"Consider it pure joy, my brothers and sisters, whenever you face trials of many kinds, because you know that the testing of your faith produces perseverance. Let perseverance finish its work so that you may be mature and complete, not lacking anything." (James 1:2-4, NIV)

James encourages us to see trials as opportunities for growth. Through challenges, our faith is tested, and perseverance is developed. This process of refining our character ultimately leads us to maturity in Christ, making us more like Him. Rather than avoiding trials, we are called to endure them with joy, knowing they have purpose.

The Last Ash: How can you shift your perspective on trials, seeing them as opportunities for growth?

The Final Sip: What trial in your life can you persevere through with joy, trusting that it's making you stronger?

January 30

Speaking with Clarity and Purpose

"Pray that I may proclaim it clearly, as I should."

(Colossians 4:4, NIV)

As men called to lead and influence, we often have opportunities to speak life into those around us—whether through mentoring, guiding our families, or being a light in our workplaces. Like Paul, we should seek God's help in ensuring our words reflect His wisdom and love, always aiming to communicate with clarity and purpose.

The Last Ash: How intentional are you about using your words to encourage and speak truth?

The Final Sip: When was the last time you asked God to guide your words in an important conversation?

January 31

Embracing God's Purpose for Your Life

"For I know the plans I have for you," declares the Lord, "plans to prosper you and not to harm you, plans to give you a hope and a future." (Jeremiah 29:11, NIV)

God has a specific purpose and plan for each of us, one that is full of hope and prosperity. Even in moments when we cannot see the full picture, we can trust that God is working for our good. His plans for us are good and will lead us to a future filled with His peace and blessings.

The Last Ash: How can you align your life today with God's purpose for you?

The Final Sip: What steps can you take to trust more fully in God's good plans for your future?

February

Battling Temptation

Let's equip ourselves with the shield of Christ

as we enter the battlefield this month.

Stay strong and confident knowing you are not alone.

February 1

Escaping the Trap of Lust

"But I tell you that anyone who looks at a woman lustfully has already committed adultery with her in his heart."
(Matthew 5:28, NIV)

Lust is a deceptive trap that begins in the mind and can lead to destructive actions. Jesus teaches that sin isn't just about outward behavior—it starts in the heart. By addressing lust at its root, we guard our thoughts and intentions, preventing sin from taking hold. The battle against lust requires intentional discipline, reliance on God's strength, and a commitment to purity. True freedom comes from surrendering our desires to Christ and filling our minds with His truth.

The Last Ash: What steps can you take to guard your heart and thoughts?

The Final Sip: How does pursuing purity reflect your commitment to Christ?

February 2

Stay Connected to the Source

"I am the vine; you are the branches. If you remain in me and I in you, you will bear much fruit; apart from me you can do nothing." (John 15:5, NIV)

Just like branches can't bear fruit unless they remain attached to the vine, we can't live lives of significance and impact without depending on Jesus daily. When we abide in Him—through prayer, Scripture, and obedience—He produces lasting fruit in our character and actions. For men called to lead and serve, this verse is a call to prioritize time with Christ, knowing that only through Him will we truly thrive and make a difference.

 The Last Ash: How can you stay more connected to Christ?

 **The Final Sip:** What fruit do you see in your life when you're walking closely with God?

February 3

Avoiding the Snare of Greed

"Then he said to them, 'Watch out! Be on your guard against all kinds of greed; life does not consist in an abundance of possessions.'" (Luke 12:15, NIV)

Greed is a deceptive trap that convinces us that more is never enough. Jesus reminds us that true life isn't measured by wealth or possessions but by our relationship with God. When we chase after material gain at the expense of our faith, we risk losing sight of what truly matters. By guarding our hearts against the love of money and focusing on generosity, we break free from the grip of greed and find lasting fulfillment in God's provision.

The Last Ash: Are you placing too much value on material possessions?

The Final Sip: How does living with gratitude free you from the grip of greed?

February 4

When Anger Controls You: Finding Freedom

"In your anger do not sin: Do not let the sun go down while you are still angry, and do not give the devil a foothold."
(Ephesians 4:26-27, NIV)

Anger itself is not a sin, but when left unchecked, it can lead to actions and attitudes that separate us from God. This passage encourages us to process anger in a way that honors Him—by addressing conflicts quickly and not allowing resentment to fester. Holding onto anger opens the door for the enemy to work in our hearts, creating division, bitterness, and unrest. Instead, surrendering our frustrations to God, seeking reconciliation, and embracing forgiveness lead to true freedom.

The Last Ash: What unresolved anger do you need to surrender to God?

The Final Sip: How can forgiveness bring you peace and freedom?

February 5

Navigating Addiction with God's Help

"No temptation has overtaken you except what is common to mankind. And God is faithful; he will not let you be tempted beyond what you can bear. But when you are tempted, he will also provide a way out so that you can endure it."
(1 Corinthians 10:13, NIV)

Addiction, whether physical, emotional, or spiritual, can feel like an inescapable trap. However, this verse reminds us that no temptation is beyond God's control, and He always provides a way out. His faithfulness assures us that we are never alone in our struggles. Overcoming addiction requires surrender—choosing to trust in God's power rather than our own.

The Last Ash: What temptation feels overwhelming in your life?

The Final Sip: How can trusting God's faithfulness give you strength to overcome?

February 6

Standing Strong Against Peer Pressure

"Do not conform to the pattern of this world, but be transformed by the renewing of your mind. Then you will be able to test and approve what God's will is—his good, pleasing and perfect will." (Romans 12:2, NIV)

Romans 12:2 calls believers to resist conforming to the world's values and instead undergo a transformation by renewing our minds through God's Word. This renewal shapes our thoughts, actions, and decisions, helping us discern what is truly good, pleasing, and perfect in God's eyes. Living in this transformed state allows us to make choices that honor God, enabling us to stand firm in our faith despite the pressures around us.

The Last Ash: How can you stay true to God's will in difficult social situations?

The Final Sip: How does renewing your mind help you resist conforming to the world?

February 7

Cultivating the Character of Christ

"But the fruit of the Spirit is love, joy, peace, forbearance, kindness, goodness, faithfulness" (Galatians 5:22, NIV)

These are not qualities we can develop on our own but are evidence of God's work in us. For men striving to live with purpose and integrity, this verse serves as a challenge to reflect Christ in every area of life—whether at home, at work, or in the community. Each of these traits represents strength under control, guiding us to respond with love instead of anger, patience instead of frustration, and faithfulness instead of compromise. When we walk by the Spirit, these fruits become visible in how we lead, serve, and influence those around us.

The Last Ash: Which fruit of the Spirit do you need to cultivate in your daily life?

The Final Sip: How can these traits shape the way you lead and influence others?

February 8

Turning to Scripture When Tempted

"Jesus answered, 'It is written: Man shall not live on bread alone, but on every word that comes from the mouth of God.'"
(Matthew 4:4, NIV)

This verse underscores the power and necessity of Scripture in the life of a believer, especially when facing temptation. Jesus, in His response to the devil, demonstrates that physical needs are not the ultimate source of life; rather, it is God's Word that nourishes and sustains us spiritually. When we turn to Scripture during times of temptation, we find guidance, strength, and truth to resist the lies and distractions of the enemy. Just as food is essential for physical survival, the Word of God is essential for spiritual health and perseverance.

The Last Ash: What Scriptures can you meditate on when facing temptation?

The Final Sip: How does God's Word equip you to overcome challenges?

February 9

The Danger of Idle Hands

"The scoundrel plots evil, and on their lips it is like a scorching fire." (Proverbs 16:27, NIV)

This verse serves as a caution against idleness, emphasizing that idleness creates space for negative thoughts and behaviors to flourish, leading to poor choices. On the other hand, engaging in purposeful work and staying active not only keeps us occupied but also helps us stay aligned with God's will. The danger lies not in rest but in prolonged inactivity that opens the door to distractions and harmful habits. By staying focused and diligent, we guard our hearts and minds from the influence of the enemy.

The Last Ash: How can you use your time wisely to glorify God? Identify daily how you might avoid idleness.

**The Final Sip:** How does purposeful work help you avoid harmful distractions?

February 10

From Envy to Contentment

"I am not saying this because I am in need, for I have learned to be content whatever the circumstances. I know what it is to be in need, and I know what it is to have plenty. I have learned the secret of being content in any and every situation, whether well fed or hungry, whether living in plenty or in want."
(Philippians 4:11-12, NIV)

Envy and discontentment often arise from comparing ourselves to others, but contentment is learned by embracing God's provision in every situation. Whether we have much or little, we can find peace in knowing that God is our ultimate provider. True contentment comes from trusting in His plans for our lives, resting in His sufficiency, and being grateful for what He has given.

The Last Ash: What areas of your life do you need to practice contentment?

The Final Sip: How can gratitude help shift your focus from envy to peace?

February 11

Be Quick to Listen, Slow to Speak

"My dear brothers and sisters, take note of this: Everyone should be quick to listen, slow to speak and slow to become angry." (James 1:19, NIV)

This verse highlights the importance of being good listeners. In a world filled with noise, taking time to listen carefully to others shows respect and understanding. By being quick to listen and slow to speak, we open the door to deeper relationships and avoid hasty words that can cause harm. In moments of frustration or disagreement, this wisdom helps us to respond with patience and gentleness rather than reacting in anger. When we pause and listen, we gain insight and clarity, which leads to better decisions and more loving interactions.

The Last Ash: How can you practice being a better listener today?

The Final Sip: How does being slow to speak prevent regretful actions?

February 12

A Heart of Generosity

"Each of you should give what you have decided in your heart to give, not reluctantly or under compulsion, for God loves a cheerful giver." (2 Corinthians 9:7, NIV)

Generosity isn't just about giving material possessions; it's about giving from a heart of love and joy. God calls us to give willingly, without hesitation or pressure, because our giving reflects our trust in His provision. When we give with a cheerful heart, we align ourselves with God's heart and experience the joy that comes from blessing others. Whether it's our time, resources, or love, generosity is an act of worship that honors God and builds up the body of Christ.

 The Last Ash: What can you give joyfully today?

 **The Final Sip:** How can giving cheerfully reflect God's love to others?

February 13

Wisdom in Action

"But the wisdom that comes from heaven is first of all pure; then peace-loving, considerate, submissive, full of mercy and good fruit, impartial and sincere." (James 3:17, NIV)

Unlike worldly wisdom, which can be self-centered and divisive, heavenly wisdom is marked by purity, peace, humility, and mercy. It seeks to build others up rather than tear them down. For men striving to lead with integrity, this verse is a guide for living and making decisions that honor God and bless others. True wisdom isn't just about knowledge—it's about applying godly principles in your actions, relationships, and leadership.

The Last Ash: Which of these traits—purity, peace, mercy, or sincerity—do you need to grow in most?

The Final Sip: How can you demonstrate godly wisdom in a current situation you're facing?

February 14

The Power of Prayer in Overcoming Temptation

"Watch and pray so that you will not fall into temptation. The spirit is willing, but the flesh is weak." (Matthew 26:41, NIV)

Jesus teaches that prayer is essential when facing temptation. While we may have the desire to resist sin, our flesh is weak, and we need God's help to overcome. Prayer strengthens our resolve, aligns our hearts with God's will, and opens us up to His power. When we face temptation, turning to God in prayer is our most powerful defense. It helps us to focus on His truth and reminds us of His promises, allowing us to stand firm in His strength.

 The Last Ash: How can you incorporate more prayer into your daily routine?

 **The Final Sip:** How does prayer empower you to resist temptation?

February 15

Fleeing from Sin

"Flee from sexual immorality. All other sins a person commits are outside the body, but whoever sins sexually, sins against their own body." (1 Corinthians 6:18, NIV)

Sin, especially sexual immorality, carries consequences that affect us deeply. This verse calls us to flee from such temptation, not engage with it. Fleeing means taking intentional steps to avoid situations that might lead us astray, recognizing that our bodies are temples of the Holy Spirit. When we choose purity, we honor God and protect ourselves from harm. Our actions reflect our reverence for God, and by fleeing from sin, we affirm our commitment to living according to His Word.

The Last Ash: What steps can you take to flee from temptation today?

The Final Sip: How does choosing purity honor God and protect you?

February 16

Replacing Temptation with Godly Habits

"Put to death, therefore, whatever belongs to your earthly nature: sexual immorality, impurity, lust, evil desires and greed, which is idolatry." (Colossians 3:5, NIV)

Paul emphasizes the importance of rejecting sinful behaviors that are rooted in our earthly nature. These desires not only hinder our spiritual growth but also separate us from the life God intends for us. By calling us to "put to death" these practices, Paul is urging believers to make a conscious decision to rid ourselves of the habits and attitudes that conflict with God's holiness.

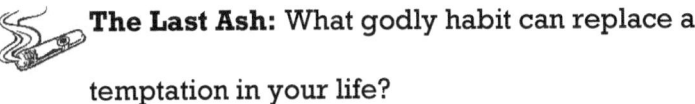**The Last Ash:** What godly habit can replace a temptation in your life?

**The Final Sip:** How does pursuing righteousness deepen your walk with God?

February 17

The Cost of Compromise

"Do not be yoked together with unbelievers. For what do righteousness and wickedness have in common? Or what fellowship can light have with darkness? What harmony is there between Christ and Belial? What does a believer have in common with an unbeliever?" (2 Corinthians 6:14-15, NIV)

Paul cautions that forming close partnerships with unbelievers can lead to spiritual conflict, as light and darkness are incompatible. Believers are called to preserve their spiritual integrity by avoiding unhealthy relationships that could pull them away from their commitment to Christ.

 **The Last Ash:** Where in your life do you need to stand firm in faith?

The Final Sip: How does staying true to God's values protect your heart?

February 18

Victory Through Christ

"But thanks be to God! He gives us the victory through our Lord Jesus Christ." (2 Corinthians 6:14-15, NIV)

Through Christ's victory over death, believers are empowered to live in triumph, knowing that their ultimate victory is secure in Him. This verse encourages Christians to embrace their new life in Christ, confident that His resurrection guarantees their own eternal victory over sin and death.

The Last Ash: What victories has God already given you? How can you return glory and share the gift with others?

The Final Sip: How does living in Christ's victory bring you peace?

February 19

Uniquely Gifted, United in Purpose

"There are different kinds of gifts, but the same Spirit distributes them." (1 Corinthians 12:4, NIV)

Gifts may differ—leadership, teaching, encouragement, serving—but they all come from the same source and are meant to work together for a greater purpose. This verse calls men to recognize and embrace their God-given abilities, not for personal gain but to serve and strengthen others. No gift is greater or less than another; they are all essential parts of God's plan. The challenge is to discover, develop, and use your gifts for His glory and the good of those around you.

 **The Last Ash:** What unique gifts or talents has God given you?

The Final Sip: How can you encourage others to use their gifts to make a greater impact?

February 20

Battling Temptation in the Digital Age

"I will not look with approval on anything that is vile. I hate what faithless people do; I will have no part in it." (Psalm 101:3, NIV)

In the digital age, we are constantly exposed to a wide range of temptations and distractions. Psalm 101:3 serves as a powerful reminder to guard what we allow into our minds and hearts, especially through digital platforms. By being intentional about what we consume, we can protect our integrity and keep our focus on purity, aligning our thoughts and actions with God's will.

The Last Ash: What changes can you make to guard your digital habits?

The Final Sip: How does honoring God with your choices protect your heart?

February 21

The Hidden Dangers of Comfort and Laziness

"How long will you lie there, you sluggard? When will you get up from your sleep? A little sleep, a little slumber, a little folding of the hands to rest—and poverty will come on you like a thief and scarcity like an armed man." (Proverbs 6:9-11, NIV)

This highlights the hidden dangers of complacency. While comfort may seem appealing, laziness ultimately leads to stagnation and negative consequences. This scripture encourages us to avoid the trap of passivity and instead embrace a proactive and disciplined lifestyle. By being diligent in our responsibilities, we honor God and avoid the slow decline that comes from neglecting our duties.

 **The Last Ash:** How can you stay productive in honoring God daily?

 **The Final Sip:** How does discipline prepare you for God's calling?

February 22

When Temptation Knocks: Preparing Your Defense

"Be alert and of sober mind. Your enemy the devil prowls around like a roaring lion looking for someone to devour."
(1 Peter 5:8, NIV)

This emphasizes the need for spiritual awareness in the face of temptation. The enemy is constantly seeking to lead us astray, and our defense lies in being watchful and prepared. Staying grounded in faith, being sober-minded, and resisting temptation are key to protecting ourselves from the destructive effects of sin. By relying on God's strength and remaining vigilant, we can stand firm against the enemy's attacks.

 The Last Ash: How can you stay alert to the enemy's schemes?

 **The Final Sip:** How does staying rooted in Christ protect you from falling?

February 23

From Shame to Redemption

"Instead of your shame you will receive a double portion, and instead of disgrace you will rejoice in your inheritance; and so you will inherit a double portion in your land, and everlasting joy will be yours." (Isaiah 61:7, NIV)

Isaiah 61:7 offers a beautiful picture of God's redemptive power. It highlights the transformation from shame to honor, illustrating that God can restore what was lost and replace feelings of disgrace with lasting joy. This verse serves as a reminder of God's faithfulness to bring healing, redemption, and restoration to those who trust in Him, turning even our darkest moments into opportunities for His grace to shine.

 The Last Ash: What shame do you need to release to God?

 **The Final Sip:** How does God's promise of redemption give you hope?

February 24

Breaking Free from the Past

"Brothers and sisters, I do not consider myself yet to have taken hold of it. But one thing I do: Forgetting what is behind and straining toward what is ahead, I press on toward the goal to win the prize for which God has called me heavenward in Christ Jesus." (Philippians 3:13-14, NIV)

In Philippians 3:13-14, Paul teaches the importance of leaving the past behind to fully embrace the future that God has prepared for us. Whether past failures or successes, they should not hinder our progress in Christ. This passage reminds us to focus on the hope of the future, knowing that God has a greater purpose for us, and to press forward with determination toward the ultimate goal of eternal life with Him. It's a call to move beyond the past and to find freedom in Christ's calling.

The Last Ash: What past regret can you leave behind today?

The Final Sip: How does focusing on God's promises help you move forward?

February 25

The Power of Saying No

"For the grace of God has appeared that offers salvation to all people. It teaches us to say 'No' to ungodliness and worldly passions, and to live self-controlled, upright and godly lives in this present age." (Titus 2:11-12, NIV)

It's not just about what we are saved from, but also about what we are saved to—living a life of self-control and godliness. The power of saying "no" to temptation comes from the grace that teaches and equips us to live according to God's will. Saying no to worldly desires is an active choice that aligns us with God's desires for our lives, enabling us to reflect His character in a world that often promotes the opposite.

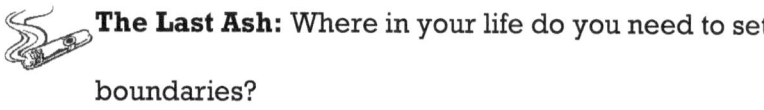
The Last Ash: Where in your life do you need to set boundaries?

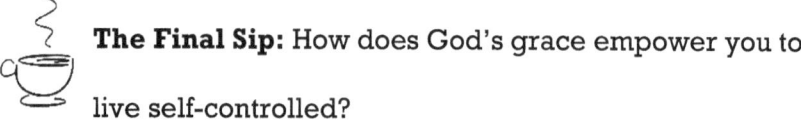
The Final Sip: How does God's grace empower you to live self-controlled?

February 26

Walking Together in Joy and Sorrow

"Rejoice with those who rejoice; mourn with those who mourn." (Romans 12:15, NIV)

Compassion requires stepping outside of ourselves to be present for others, celebrating others victories and standing with them in their struggles. For men striving to lead and support others, this verse reminds us that true strength is found in being emotionally available. Whether it's rejoicing in someone's success or offering comfort during hardship, we're called to walk alongside others with understanding and love.

The Last Ash: How can you be more intentional about celebrating others' successes and supporting them?

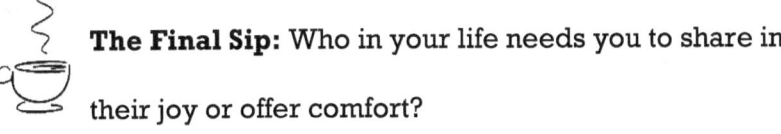

The Final Sip: Who in your life needs you to share in their joy or offer comfort?

February 27

Resisting the Devil's Schemes

"Submit yourselves, then, to God. Resist the devil, and he will flee from you." (James 4:7, NIV)

Resisting the devil requires both humility and strength. By submitting to God, we place ourselves under His protection and authority, making it harder for the devil to influence us. When we stand firm in our faith and resist temptation, we activate God's power in our lives. The promise that the devil will flee is a reminder that our resistance, grounded in God's strength, has the power to overcome evil. The key to this victory is a heart surrendered to God's will, trusting in His protection and guidance.

 The Last Ash: What steps can you take to submit fully to God?

 **The Final Sip:** How does drawing near to God protect you from evil?

February 28

Triumphing Over Trials

"No, in all these things we are more than conquerors through him who loved us." (Romans 8:37, NIV)

In the face of life's trials, Romans 8:37 reminds believers of their victory in Christ. It declares that we are not just survivors of hardship, but more than conquerors. Through Christ's love and strength, we have the power to overcome every challenge, knowing that nothing can separate us from His love. This triumphant perspective shifts our focus from the difficulty of trials to the strength we receive through Christ, enabling us to face challenges with hope and resilience.

The Last Ash: How can you see your trials as opportunities to reflect Christ?

The Final Sip: How does knowing you are a conqueror in Christ affect your outlook?

March

Strengthening Your Walk

This month we put into practice the commands of Scripture.

Through intentional daily devotions, growth begins.

March 1

Building Daily Spiritual Habits

"In the morning, Lord, you hear my voice; in the morning I lay my requests before you and wait expectantly." (Psalm 5:3, NIV)

Psalm 5:3 encourages establishing a daily habit of dedicating time in the morning to connect with God. It suggests that the first moments of the day should be spent in prayer, aligning ourselves with God's will. This daily practice not only invites God's presence into our lives but also fosters a mindset of dependence on Him, setting a foundation of peace and purpose that carries through the rest of the day.

 **The Last Ash:** What spiritual habit can you begin to implement in your daily life?

The Final Sip: How does spending time with God each day transform your heart?

March 2

Guarding Your Heart and Mind

"Reject every kind of evil." (1 Thessalonians 5:22, NIV)

Rejecting evil means more than avoiding obvious wrongdoing—it involves guarding our hearts, thoughts, and actions from influences that can harm our spiritual walk. As men, we are constantly faced with choices that can either strengthen or weaken our character. This verse reminds us to be proactive in identifying and turning away from anything that doesn't align with God's standards, choosing instead what is good, true, and honorable.

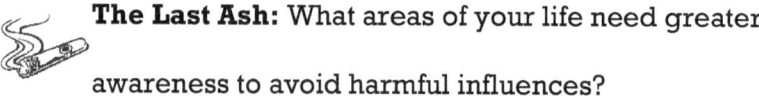 **The Last Ash:** What areas of your life need greater awareness to avoid harmful influences?

 **The Final Sip:** How can you set boundaries that help you reject what is wrong and pursue what is good?

March 3

Finding Strength in the Psalms

"God is our refuge and strength, an ever-present help in trouble. Therefore we will not fear, though the earth give way and the mountains fall into the heart of the sea, though its waters roar and foam and the mountains quake with their surging." (Psalm 46:1-3, NIV)

God is our ultimate source of strength and security. The imagery of the earth shaking and mountains crumbling reflects the most extreme and uncontrollable forces, yet the psalmist assures us that we need not fear. In times of distress, turning to God provides both emotional and spiritual fortitude.

The Last Ash: Ask for help. In what areas of your life do you need God's strength?

The Final Sip: How does meditating on the Psalms give you comfort in tough times?

March 4

Walking with God Through the Valleys

"Even though I walk through the darkest valley, I will fear no evil, for you are with me; your rod and your staff, they comfort me." (Psalm 23:4, NIV)

Psalm 23:4 emphasizes that God's presence isn't just a comfort during the good times but also during life's darkest and most difficult moments. The "valley" represents life's trials, where fear and uncertainty often arise. Yet, with God's guidance, we can walk through these valleys with courage. His "rod" and "staff" represent tools of protection and guidance, ensuring that even in our lowest points, we are not alone.

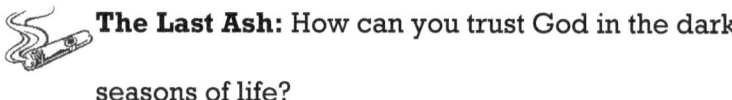**The Last Ash:** How can you trust God in the dark seasons of life?

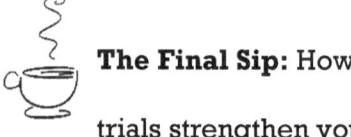**The Final Sip:** How does walking with God through trials strengthen your faith?

March 5

Faith in Action: More Than Words

"In the same way, faith by itself, if it is not accompanied by action, is dead." (James 2:17, NIV)

Real faith is shown through what we do, not just what we say. Faith should be active and alive, impacting our daily actions and decisions. When we claim to have faith in God, it should be evident in how we treat others, how we live our lives, and how we align our actions with God's will. Faith isn't a passive belief but an active force that should compel us to live out God's love and truth in tangible ways.

The Last Ash: What actions can you take today to demonstrate your faith?

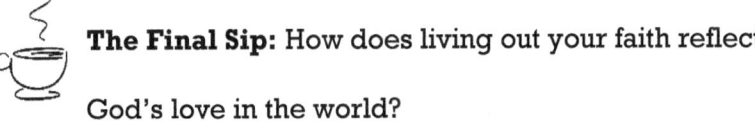

The Final Sip: How does living out your faith reflect God's love in the world?

March 6

The Reward of Obedience

"If you fully obey the Lord your God and carefully follow all his commands I give you today, the Lord your God will set you high above all the nations on earth. All these blessings will come on you and accompany you if you obey the Lord your God." (Deuteronomy 28:1-2, NIV)

Obedience isn't just about following rules; it's about trusting in God's wisdom and recognizing that His commands are for our benefit. These blessings aren't just material but encompass peace, favor, and a life aligned with God's purpose. While obedience may require sacrifice or discipline, it is the pathway to a life filled with God's promises.

The Last Ash: In what areas do you need to walk in obedience to God's Word?

The Final Sip: How does obedience bring blessings into your life?

March 7

What It Means to Be a Servant Leader

"For even the Son of Man did not come to be served, but to serve, and to give his life as a ransom for many."
(Mark 10:45, NIV)

True leadership in God's eyes is about serving others, not elevating oneself. Jesus modeled this perfectly by willingly offering His life for the benefit of humanity, showcasing the ultimate act of service. In a world that often values power and status, Jesus' words challenge us to lead with compassion, empathy, and a heart to meet the needs of others. Servant leadership is about fostering relationships, guiding through example, and seeking the welfare of others above personal gain.

 The Last Ash: How can you serve others with a heart like Christ's?

 The Final Sip: How does leading through service impact those around you?

March 8

The Importance of Sabbath Rest

"Remember the Sabbath day by keeping it holy. Six days you shall labor and do all your work, but the seventh day is a sabbath to the Lord your God. On it you shall not do any work, neither you, nor your son or daughter, nor your male or female servant, nor your animals, nor any foreigner residing in your towns." (Exodus 20:8-10, NIV)

The Sabbath is a gift from God, meant for restoration and worship. It's a reminder that our values and purpose don't come from our work but from our Creator. In the hustle of life, it's easy to overlook the need for rest, but God designed the Sabbath as a deliberate pause to recharge physically, emotionally, and spiritually.

The Last Ash: How can you set aside time for rest and renewal?

The Final Sip: How does honoring the Sabbath refresh your spirit and body?

March 9

Aligning Your Plans with God's Purpose

"Commit to the Lord whatever you do, and he will establish your plans." (Proverbs 16:3, NIV)

When we submit our plans to God, we acknowledge that His wisdom surpasses our own, and we trust in His guidance over our desires. Proverbs 16:3 teaches that our work and efforts should not be solely driven by personal gain, but rather by a commitment to God's direction. By dedicating our plans to God, we invite Him into our decision-making process, ensuring that our goals align with His greater purposes.

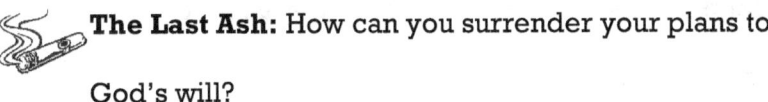**The Last Ash:** How can you surrender your plans to God's will?

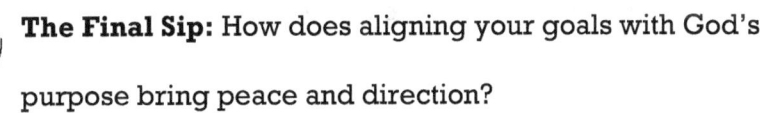**The Final Sip:** How does aligning your goals with God's purpose bring peace and direction?

March 10

Turning to God in Stressful Times

"Come to me, all you who are weary and burdened, and I will give you rest. Take my yoke upon you and learn from me, for I am gentle and humble in heart, and you will find rest for your souls. For my yoke is easy and my burden is light."
(Matthew 11:28-30, NIV)

In moments of stress and weariness, Matthew 11:28-30 reminds us that we have a place to turn for rest and renewal—Jesus Himself. The invitation is clear: come to Him, bring your burdens, and allow Him to restore your soul. Jesus offers not just rest from physical labor but from the emotional and spiritual burdens we carry. The yoke of Jesus is not a heavy burden; rather, it is one of grace and peace.

The Last Ash: What burdens do you need to surrender to Jesus today?

The Final Sip: How does coming to Jesus for rest transform your soul?

March 11

Living Out the Fruit of the Spirit

"But the fruit of the Spirit is love, joy, peace, forbearance, kindness, goodness, faithfulness, gentleness and self-control. Against such things there is no law." (Galatians 5:22-23, NIV)

These qualities—love, joy, peace, patience, kindness, goodness, faithfulness, gentleness, and self-control—are the fruit of a life lived in obedience to God. They are evidence of God's work in us, and they distinguish us as His followers. The fruit of the Spirit is not something we can produce on our own; it is the result of allowing the Holy Spirit to guide and empower us.

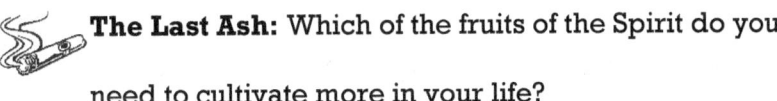 **The Last Ash:** Which of the fruits of the Spirit do you need to cultivate more in your life?

 **The Final Sip:** How can the fruit of the Spirit influence your relationships and daily interactions?

March 12

The Importance of Gratitude in Every Circumstance

"Do not be anxious about anything, but in every situation, by prayer and petition, with thanksgiving, present your requests to God. And the peace of God, which transcends all understanding, will guard your hearts and your minds in Christ Jesus." (Philippians 4:6-7, NIV)

Gratitude shifts our focus from our worries to God's provision and faithfulness. By acknowledging God's goodness, even in difficult times, we invite His peace to guard our hearts and minds. Gratitude also cultivates trust, allowing us to release anxiety and replace it with a confident expectation that God will work everything out for our good.

 The Last Ash: How can you incorporate gratitude into your prayer life, even in tough times?

 **The Final Sip:** How does gratitude change your perspective on challenges?

March 13

The Call to Humility

"Do nothing out of selfish ambition or vain conceit. Rather, in humility value others above yourselves, not looking to your own interests but each of you to the interests of the others." (Philippians 2:3-4, NIV)

Humility is a core trait that reflects the heart of Christ. True humility requires us to place the needs and interests of others before our own, which is countercultural in a world that often encourages self-promotion. Humility leads to healthy relationships, mutual respect, and an attitude that seeks to serve rather than to be served. Jesus demonstrated the ultimate humility when He left His throne in heaven and came to serve humanity, ultimately laying down His life for us.

The Last Ash: How can you practice humility in your relationships and daily actions?

The Final Sip: How does valuing others above yourself shape your life and interactions?

March 14

The Blessings of Generosity

"Remember this: Whoever sows sparingly will also reap sparingly, and whoever sows generously will also reap generously. Each of you should give what you have decided in your heart to give, not reluctantly or under compulsion, for God loves a cheerful giver." (2 Corinthians 9:6-7, NIV)

When we give generously, whether of our time, talents, or resources, we reflect God's generous nature. God doesn't just look at the amount we give, but the attitude of our hearts. Cheerful giving brings blessing both to the giver and the receiver. Generosity is an expression of our trust in God's provision, and it opens the door for His continued blessing in our lives.

The Last Ash: What can you give generously today, whether it's time, resources, or encouragement?

The Final Sip: How does a cheerful heart in giving reflect God's love and provision?

March 15

Resting in God's Sovereignty

"For my thoughts are not your thoughts, neither are your ways my ways, declares the Lord. As the heavens are higher than the earth, so are my ways higher than your ways and my thoughts than your thoughts." (Isaiah 55:8-9, NIV)

There will be times in life when we don't understand why certain things happen, but we can trust that God's ways are perfect. His plans are far greater than anything we can imagine, and His wisdom is beyond our comprehension. This passage calls us to rest in the sovereignty of God, knowing that He is in control, even when things seem uncertain or difficult.

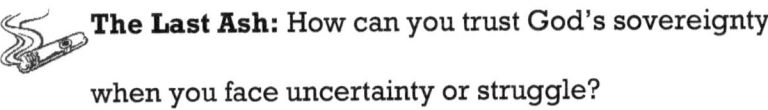**The Last Ash:** How can you trust God's sovereignty when you face uncertainty or struggle?

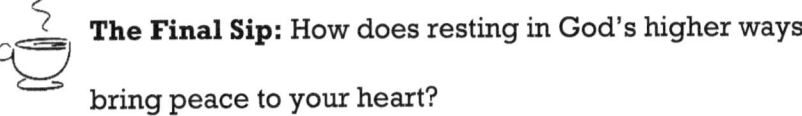**The Final Sip:** How does resting in God's higher ways bring peace to your heart?

March 16

Gifts with a Purpose

"Now to each one the manifestation of the Spirit is given for the common good." (1 Corinthians 12:7, NIV)

The gifts of the Spirit are meant to strengthen, encourage, and build up others in the community of faith. Whether your gift is leadership, service, wisdom, or encouragement, it's not just for you; it's a tool to bless others. As men called to lead and serve, this verse challenges us to use what God has given us to make a meaningful impact on those around us and to contribute to something greater than ourselves.

 **The Last Ash:** How are you using your God-given gifts to benefit others?

The Final Sip: Who in your life can you support and build up with your spiritual gifts?

March 17

Being a Man of Your Word

"All you need to say is simply 'Yes' or 'No'; anything beyond this comes from the evil one." (Matthew 5:37, NIV)

Jesus calls us to a higher standard of truthfulness and reliability. In a world full of empty promises and deceitful words, this teaching emphasizes the need for personal integrity. When we say "Yes," it should be a reflection of our intention to follow through, and when we say "No," it should be firm and final. Our words are powerful, and they should align with our actions, as this is the foundation of trustworthiness.

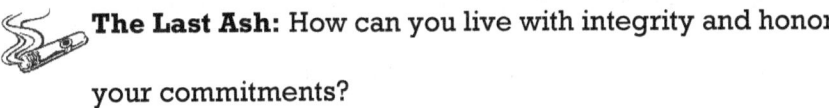 **The Last Ash:** How can you live with integrity and honor your commitments?

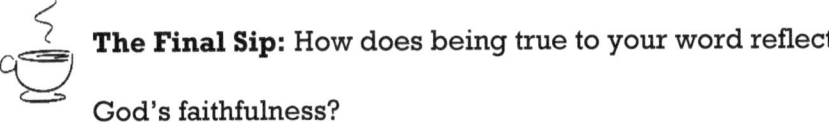 **The Final Sip:** How does being true to your word reflect God's faithfulness?

March 18

Encouraging Others in Their Walk

"And let us consider how we may spur one another on toward love and good deeds, not giving up meeting together, as some are in the habit of doing, but encouraging one another—and all the more as you see the Day approaching."
(Hebrews 10:24-25, NIV)

The Christian walk is not meant to be lived in isolation; we are called to be part of a supportive community that helps each other grow in faith. This is not a passive activity, but an active, ongoing process of inspiring others toward spiritual growth and service. Encouraging others is not just about offering support during tough times, but also about building each other up to live out the love and good works that reflect Christ's character.

The Last Ash: How can you encourage others in their faith today?

The Final Sip: How does building up others strengthen the body of Christ?

March 19

Finding Joy in Difficult Seasons

"Consider it pure joy, my brothers and sisters, whenever you face trials of many kinds, because you know that the testing of your faith produces perseverance." (James 1:2-3, NIV)

James flips the typical human response to suffering on its head. Instead of reacting with frustration or despair when facing difficulties, James challenges believers to view trials through the lens of faith, seeing them as a means to develop perseverance and character. God does not waste pain; rather, He uses challenges to refine us and draw us closer to Him.

The Last Ash: What trial are you facing, and how can you find joy in it?

The Final Sip: How does seeing trials as opportunities strengthen your faith?

March 20

Knowing God Through His Word

"Your word is a lamp for my feet, a light on my path."
(Psalm 119:105, NIV)

Psalm 119:105 highlights the central role of Scripture in the life of a believer. Just as a lamp guides us through a dark path, God's Word directs us when we face uncertainty or difficulty. In times of confusion, we often look for answers in the world around us, but the psalmist reminds us that the Bible offers the clearest and most reliable guidance. By reading and meditating on Scripture, we gain insight into who God is and what He desires for our lives.

 **The Last Ash:** How can you commit to knowing God more deeply through His Word?

The Final Sip: How does Scripture light your path and guide your steps?

March 21

Stewardship: Managing What God Gives You

"Each of you should use whatever gift you have received to serve others, as faithful stewards of God's grace in its various forms." (1 Peter 4:10, NIV)

The concept of stewardship extends beyond merely managing material possessions. It encompasses the responsible use of all gifts—spiritual, physical, and relational—that God has entrusted to us. The variety of gifts mentioned implies that God has equipped each person uniquely, and there is no room for comparison or self-centeredness in the way we use them.

 **The Last Ash:** How can you be a faithful steward of the gifts God has entrusted to you?

The Final Sip: How does stewardship reflect your gratitude to God?

March 22

Pursuing Holiness in a Broken World

"But just as he who called you is holy, so be holy in all you do; for it is written: 'Be holy, because I am holy.'"
(1 Peter 1:15-16, NIV)

Holiness is not just about external actions but involves a transformation of the heart, choosing to live according to God's standards rather than conforming to the world's sinful patterns. Though challenging, this pursuit is made possible by the Holy Spirit's work in believers' lives. Reflecting God's holiness is a response to His grace, aligning thoughts, actions, and desires with His will.

 **The Last Ash:** How can you pursue holiness in the midst of challenges?

The Final Sip: How does living a holy life reflect God's character to the world?

March 23

The Freedom of Forgiveness

"Be kind and compassionate to one another, forgiving each other, just as in Christ God forgave you." (Ephesians 4:32, NIV)

Forgiveness is essential to pursuing holiness, as it frees individuals from the bitterness and anger that hinder spiritual growth. While forgiveness doesn't mean excusing wrongdoing, it reflects God's grace and mercy, allowing His love to flow through us. By forgiving others, believers break free from the burdens of the past and align their lives with God's will, demonstrating His transformative power in a broken world.

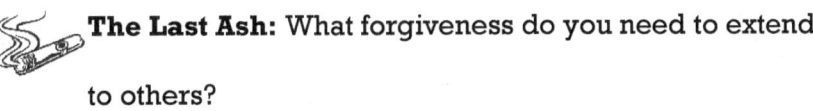
The Last Ash: What forgiveness do you need to extend to others?

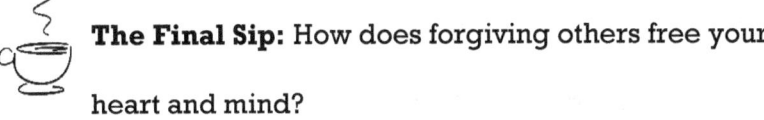
The Final Sip: How does forgiving others free your heart and mind?

March 24

Speaking Life in Every Situation

"The tongue has the power of life and death, and those who love it will eat its fruit." (Proverbs 18:21, NIV)

Our words hold immense power—they can build up or tear down, heal or wound, bring hope or spread despair. When we align our words with God's truth, we cultivate a spirit of love, wisdom, and grace, bearing the fruit of life-giving speech. Today, choose to speak words that uplift, inspire, and reflect the goodness of God.

The Last Ash: How can you speak words of life and encouragement today?

The Final Sip: How does speaking life reflect God's love in your conversations?

March 25

Accountability in the Fight Against Sin

"Brothers and sisters, if someone is caught in a sin, you who live by the Spirit should restore that person gently. But watch yourselves, or you also may be tempted. Carry each other's burdens, and in this way you will fulfill the law of Christ." (Galatians 6:1-2, NIV)

Accountability is a vital part of our walk with Christ. When a fellow believer stumbles, our role is not to condemn but to encourage them back to righteousness while guarding our own hearts against temptation. Walking in community means sharing each other's burdens, offering grace, and upholding the truth in love. True accountability strengthens our faith, fosters humility, and helps us all grow closer to Christ.

The Last Ash: How can you hold others accountable with gentleness and humility today?

The Final Sip: How does helping others carry their burdens fulfill the law of Christ?

March 26

True Greatness through Service

"Not so with you. Instead, whoever wants to become great among you must be your servant." (Mark 10:43, NIV)

Jesus calls us to lead with humility and a servant's heart. True strength is found not in being above others but in lifting them up. For men seeking to make a lasting impact, this verse is a powerful reminder that greatness comes through selflessness and putting others' needs before our own. When we lead by serving, we reflect the heart of Christ and leave a legacy of genuine influence and love.

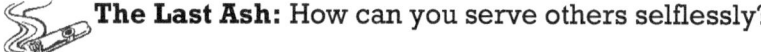**The Last Ash:** How can you serve others selflessly?

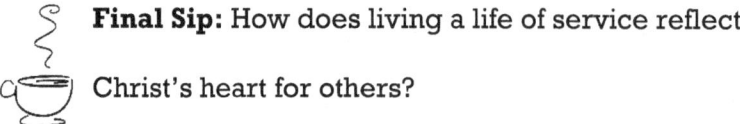**Final Sip:** How does living a life of service reflect Christ's heart for others?

March 27

Living Out Your Faith Boldly

"Now, Lord, consider their threats and enable your servants to speak your word with great boldness." (Acts 4:29, NIV)

The apostles did not pray for their circumstances to change, but for the strength to continue living and speaking the truth of the gospel. As believers, we are also called to be bold in our faith, sharing the hope of Christ with others, even in the face of opposition. Boldness does not mean being brash or confrontational, but rather standing firm in the truth and speaking out when it is difficult. God promises to equip us with the strength we need, and His Spirit empowers us to be bold witnesses for Him.

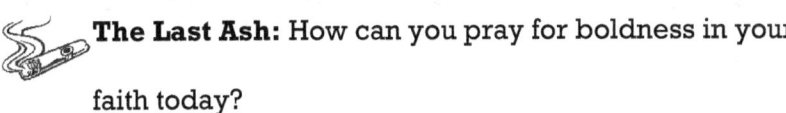 **The Last Ash:** How can you pray for boldness in your faith today?

 **The Final Sip:** How does living boldly for Christ impact those around you?

March 28

Reflecting Christ in Our Actions

"Whoever claims to live in him must live as Jesus did."

(1 John 2:6, NIV)

Living as Jesus lived is the ultimate goal for every believer. Jesus' life was marked by compassion, humility, and a commitment to doing the will of the Father. He healed the sick, comforted the broken-hearted, and always sought the good of others, even at great personal cost. As His followers, we are called to reflect those same qualities in our own lives. It's easy to become distracted by the demands and busyness of life, but this verse calls us back to the central task of reflecting Christ in all we do.

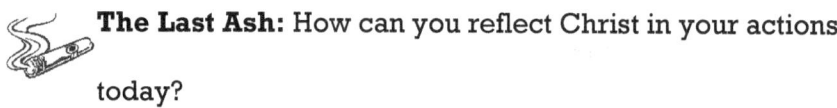 **The Last Ash:** How can you reflect Christ in your actions today?

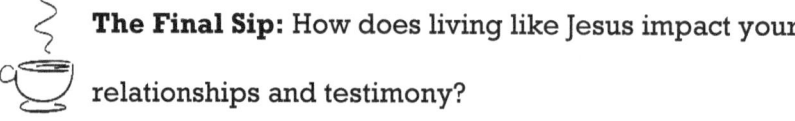 **The Final Sip:** How does living like Jesus impact your relationships and testimony?

March 29

Finding Strength in God's Presence

"You make known to me the path of life; you will fill me with joy in your presence, with eternal pleasures at your right hand." (Psalm 16:11, NIV)

David expresses in this verse that God's presence is the source of all true joy and fulfillment. This joy is not based on circumstances but on the assurance that God is with us, guiding our path, and filling our hearts with His peace and contentment. In the presence of God, we find not only joy but strength for the journey. Life's challenges can leave us weary, but when we enter into God's presence through prayer, worship, and His Word, He replenishes our souls.

 The Last Ash: How can you intentionally seek God's presence today?

 **The Final Sip:** How does God's presence strengthen and refresh you?

March 30

Trusting God's Timing

"Let us not become weary in doing good, for at the proper time we will reap a harvest if we do not give up." (Galatians 6:9, NIV)

We often want instant results, but this verse encourages us not to give up, even when the reward seems distant. Just as a farmer waits patiently for his harvest, we must remain faithful in doing good, knowing that God is working behind the scenes. For men striving to lead and make an impact, this verse is a powerful reminder that every effort sown in faith will bear fruit in God's time

.

 **The Last Ash:** What is one area of your life where you need to trust God's timing more fully?

The Final Sip: How can you stay motivated to keep doing good, even when the results aren't immediate?

March 31

Living a Life of Thankfulness

"Give thanks in all circumstances; for this is God's will for you in Christ Jesus." (1 Thessalonians 5:18, NIV)

Thankfulness is not merely an occasional response to blessings, but a continual attitude that reflects our trust in God. Paul writes that we are to give thanks in all circumstances, not because of the circumstances themselves, but because we trust that God is at work in every situation for our good. This doesn't mean we are thankful for the difficulties themselves, but that we recognize that God is using them to shape us, refine us, and bring about His purposes. A heart of gratitude acknowledges that, regardless of the trials we face, God is good, and He is faithful.

The Last Ash: How can you cultivate a heart of gratitude today?

The Final Sip: How does living a life of thankfulness transform your perspective?

April

Leadership in Life and Family

This month we will focus on foundational leadership, and it starts with you.

April 1

Leading Like Jesus: Servant Leadership

"Not so with you. Instead, whoever wants to become great among you must be your servant, and whoever wants to be first must be your slave—just as the Son of Man did not come to be served, but to serve, and to give his life as a ransom for many." (Matthew 20:26-28, NIV)

Jesus teaches that true leadership is not about power or dominance but about serving others. He contrasts worldly leadership, where rulers exercise authority over people, with godly leadership, which is marked by humility and service. Jesus sets the ultimate example by stating that He came not to be served, but to serve and to give His life as a ransom for many.

The Last Ash: How can you model servant leadership in your role today?

The Final Sip: How does leading with humility and service change your influence on others?

April 2

Building Your House on the Rock

"Therefore everyone who hears these words of mine and puts them into practice is like a wise man who built his house on the rock. The rain came down, the streams rose, and the winds blew and beat against that house; yet it did not fall, because it had its foundation on the rock." (Matthew 7:24-25, NIV)

Building your life on the foundation of God's Word provides strength and stability in the face of life's uncertainties. Just as a strong foundation keeps a house standing through storms, a faith rooted in Christ helps believers remain steadfast through difficulties. Obedience to God's teachings is not just about hearing but applying His wisdom daily, ensuring that no matter what trials arise, our lives remain anchored in His truth.

**The Last Ash:** What foundation are you building your life and family on?

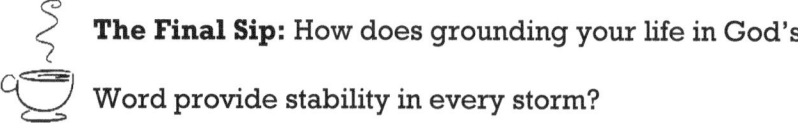**The Final Sip:** How does grounding your life in God's Word provide stability in every storm?

April 3

A Father's Influence: Leaving a Legacy of Faith

"Start children off on the way they should go, and even when they are old they will not turn from it." (Proverbs 22:6, NIV)

A father's influence plays a crucial role in shaping a child's faith and values. Teaching children about God's truth, modeling integrity, and nurturing their spiritual growth create a lasting legacy that extends beyond one generation. While challenges may arise, a foundation built on faith provides children with the wisdom and strength to navigate life's trials, reinforcing the importance of godly leadership within the family.

The Last Ash: How can you intentionally shape the faith of the next generation?

The Final Sip: How does leaving a legacy of faith impact your children and those around you?

April 4

Husbands Who Lead with Love

"Husbands, love your wives, just as Christ loved the church and gave himself up for her." (Ephesians 5:25, NIV)

Biblical leadership in marriage is not about dominance but about selfless love. A husband who leads with love mirrors Christ's devotion to the Church, prioritizing his wife's needs, offering support, and fostering a relationship built on trust and sacrifice. This kind of love strengthens the marriage, cultivates unity, and creates an environment where both spouses can thrive in faith and purpose.

The Last Ash: In what ways can you love your spouse sacrificially today?

The Final Sip: How does leading with love reflect Christ's love for the Church?

April 5

Standing Firm in Your Convictions

"Be on your guard; stand firm in the faith; be courageous; be strong. Do everything in love." (1 Corinthians 16:13-14, NIV)

Standing firm in your convictions requires both strength and love. In a world that often challenges biblical values, it is essential to remain steadfast in faith while responding to opposition with grace. True conviction is not about stubbornness but about being deeply rooted in God's truth, allowing His wisdom to guide decisions and actions. When faith is expressed with both courage and love, it becomes a powerful testimony to those around us.

The Last Ash: Where do you need to stand firm in your faith and convictions?

The Final Sip: How does standing firm in your beliefs strengthen your relationship with God and others?

April 6

Modeling Faith for Your Children

"These commandments that I give you today are to be on your hearts. Impress them on your children. Talk about them when you sit at home and when you walk along the road, when you lie down and when you get up." (Deuteronomy 6:6-7, NIV)

Modeling faith for children is not just about teaching biblical principles but living them out consistently. When parents demonstrate a love for God through their actions, words, and decisions, they create a foundation for their children to develop their own faith. Faith should be woven into everyday life—whether through prayer, scripture, or showing Christ-like love—so that children see and experience God's presence in their home.

 The Last Ash: How can you incorporate faith into your daily routine with your children?

 **The Final Sip:** How does modeling faith in everyday life help your children develop their own relationship with God?

April 7

The Responsibility of Leadership

"Not many of you should become teachers, my fellow believers, because you know that we who teach will be judged more strictly." (James 3:1, NIV)

Leadership is not just about authority but about accountability. Those in leadership positions, whether in the church, family, or workplace, must recognize the impact of their words and decisions. A leader's guidance can shape the faith and character of others, making it crucial to lead with wisdom, humility, and integrity. By seeking God's direction and living by His truth, leaders can fulfill their role responsibly and serve as a Christlike example to those they influence.

The Last Ash: How can you embrace the responsibility that comes with leadership?

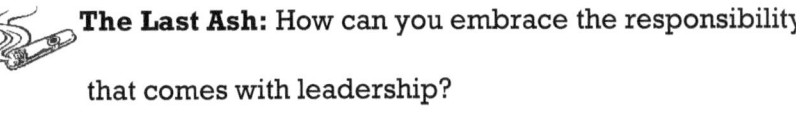

The Final Sip: How does recognizing the weight of leadership influence the way you lead others?

April 8

Walking in Wisdom in Your Decisions

"Trust in the Lord with all your heart and lean not on your own understanding; in all your ways submit to him, and he will make your paths straight." (Proverbs 3:5-6, NIV)

Making wise decisions requires surrendering control to God and seeking His guidance. Human understanding is limited, but God's wisdom is perfect. Trusting Him means leaning on His Word, praying for discernment, and being open to His leading. When we acknowledge God in our choices, He faithfully directs our steps, ensuring that we walk in alignment with His will.

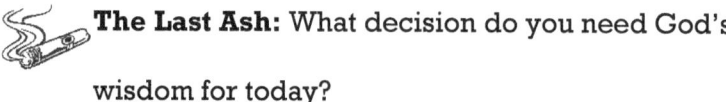**The Last Ash:** What decision do you need God's wisdom for today?

**The Final Sip:** How does trusting in God's guidance lead to better, more faithful decisions?

April 9

Balancing Work and Family God's Way

"There is a time for everything, and a season for every activity under the heavens: a time to be born and a time to die, a time to plant and a time to uproot, a time to kill and a time to heal, a time to tear down and a time to build, a time to weep and a time to laugh, a time to mourn and a time to dance, a time to scatter stones and a time to gather them, a time to embrace and a time to refrain from embracing." (Ecclesiastes 3:1-8, NIV)

Balancing work and family require understanding priorities and trusting God's timing. It is easy to get caught up in work demands or personal ambitions, but God calls us to live with intentionality. By seeking His wisdom, we can establish boundaries, cherish family moments, and fulfill our work duties without neglecting the most important relationships in our lives.

The Last Ash: How can you balance your work responsibilities with your family commitments?

The Final Sip: How does recognizing that each season of life has its purpose help you prioritize well?

April 10

Strength in Weakness

"But he said to me, 'My grace is sufficient for you, for my power is made perfect in weakness.' Therefore I will boast all the more gladly of my weaknesses, so that the power of Christ may rest upon me." (2 Corinthians 12:9, NIV)

When we face weakness, whether physical, emotional, or spiritual, we are reminded that we do not have to rely on our own abilities. God's grace is more than enough to sustain us and equip us for the challenges we face. Embracing weakness is an invitation to depend on God's strength and experience His power at work within us.

The Last Ash: How can you embrace your weakness and rely on God's strength?

The Final Sip: How does God's grace transform our weaknesses into opportunities for His power to be displayed?

April 11

Embracing God's Plan for Your Life

"For I know the plans I have for you," declares the Lord, "plans to prosper you and not to harm you, plans to give you a hope and a future." (Jeremiah 29:11, NIV)

Trusting in God's plan requires surrendering our own desires and ambitions to His will. While we may not always understand His timing or methods, we can rest assured that He is guiding us toward a purpose greater than we can imagine. When we align our hearts with His plans, we find peace, hope, and fulfillment in the journey.

The Last Ash: How can you embrace God's plan for your life, even when it doesn't look the way you expected?

The Final Sip: How does trusting God's plan give you hope for the future?

April 12

The Power of Forgiveness

"For if you forgive other people when they sin against you, your heavenly Father will also forgive you. But if you do not forgive others their sins, your Father will not forgive your sins." (Matthew 6:14-15, NIV)

Forgiveness doesn't mean condoning wrongdoing, but it frees us from the chains of anger and hurt. By forgiving others, we reflect God's grace and mercy toward us. It is through forgiveness that we experience healing, peace, and reconciliation in our relationships. As we forgive, we are reminded of how much God has forgiven us, inspiring us to extend that same grace to others.

The Last Ash: Who do you need to forgive in your life today?

The Final Sip: How does forgiving others release you from bitterness and draw you closer to God?

April 13

Living Out the Great Commission

"Therefore go and make disciples of all nations, baptizing them in the name of the Father and of the Son and of the Holy Spirit, and teaching them to obey everything I have commanded you. And surely I am with you always, to the very end of the age." (Matthew 28:19-20, NIV)

Living out the Great Commission means actively participating in God's mission to bring others into His kingdom. Whether through personal relationships, acts of service, or spreading the message of salvation, we have the privilege of being His ambassadors. Jesus promises to be with us always, empowering us to fulfill this calling with courage and love.

The Last Ash: How can you participate in fulfilling the Great Commission in your everyday life?

The Final Sip: How does knowing that Jesus is with you always give you confidence in sharing your faith?

April 14

Pursuing Peace with Others

"If it is possible, as far as it depends on you, live at peace with everyone." (Romans 12:18, NIV)

Living at peace with others requires humility, patience, and a willingness to forgive. While we cannot control others' actions, we can control how we respond. When we seek peace instead of conflict, we reflect God's love and bring healing to broken relationships. Peace is not merely the absence of conflict but a pursuit of unity and reconciliation, grounded in God's grace.

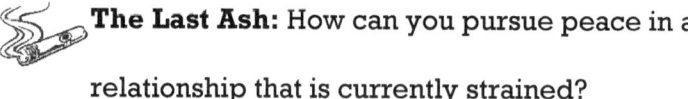 **The Last Ash:** How can you pursue peace in a relationship that is currently strained?

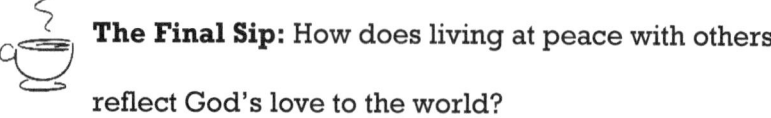 **The Final Sip:** How does living at peace with others reflect God's love to the world?

April 15

The Value of True Friendship

"As iron sharpens iron, so one person sharpens another." (Proverbs 27:17, NIV)

True friendships are built on trust, honesty, and mutual growth. They are relationships where both individuals help one another become more like Christ. Just as iron sharpens iron, we are called to help each other develop spiritually, emotionally, and mentally. A strong, godly friendship not only provides support in times of need but also helps us stay focused on our purpose in Christ.

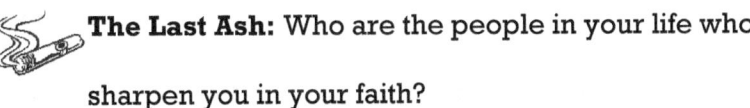

The Last Ash: Who are the people in your life who sharpen you in your faith?

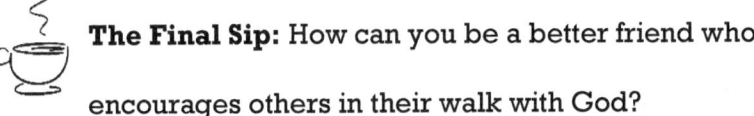

The Final Sip: How can you be a better friend who encourages others in their walk with God?

April 16

Choosing Good Over Revenge

"Make sure that nobody pays back wrong for wrong, but always strive to do what is good for each other and for everyone else." (1 Thessalonians 5:15, NIV)

It's easy to justify getting even when we've been wronged, but this verse calls men to a higher standard. Doing good to others, even when it's undeserved, reflects the character of Christ. This kind of response requires strength, self-control, and a focus on the greater good. It's not about letting others take advantage of us but about choosing integrity and love over bitterness and revenge.

 **The Last Ash:** How can you respond with grace instead of retaliation when someone wrongs you?

The Final Sip: What practical ways can you strive to do good for others?

April 17

Leading with Integrity

"The integrity of the upright guides them, but the unfaithful are destroyed by their duplicity." (Proverbs 11:3, NIV)

Integrity is the cornerstone of effective leadership. A leader who operates with honesty, transparency, and moral character earns trust and respect from others. In contrast, when a leader compromises on integrity, they risk their credibility and the stability of their influence. Leading with integrity involves staying true to one's values and being accountable, even when facing temptations or challenges. It ultimately ensures that leadership decisions align with both personal convictions and God's principles.

The Last Ash: Where do you need to strengthen your integrity as a leader?

The Final Sip: How does integrity in leadership build trust and honor God?

April 18

Teaching the Next Generation

"We will not hide them from their descendants; we will tell the next generation the praiseworthy deeds of the Lord, His power, and the wonders He has done." (Psalm 78:4, NIV)

Teaching the next generation about God's faithfulness and truth is a vital responsibility of believers. By sharing God's works, commandments, and promises, parents and leaders provide a firm foundation for children to build their lives upon. The next generation must not only know about God but also experience His love and power. Through intentional teaching, both through words and actions, we can pass on a legacy of faith, helping the younger generation develop a strong and lasting relationship with God.

 The Last Ash: How can you share your faith with the next generation today?

 **The Final Sip:** How does investing in the spiritual growth of others leave a lasting impact?

April 19

Strength in Surrender

"That is why, for Christ's sake, I delight in weaknesses, in insults, in hardships, in persecutions, in difficulties. For when I am weak, then I am strong." (2 Corinthians 12:10, NIV)

Surrendering to God's will and acknowledging our weaknesses allows His strength to shine through. While the world often associates strength with self-reliance, true power comes through humility and trust in God. When we let go of our own control and embrace our limitations, we create space for God's grace and power to work in and through us. Surrender doesn't mean weakness—it is in yielding to God that we find the strength to endure, grow, and fulfill His purposes.

The Last Ash: What area of your life do you need to surrender to God today?

The Final Sip: How does surrendering to God's strength transform your leadership and faith?

April 20

Leading Through Adversity

"Blessed is the one who perseveres under trial because, having stood the test, that person will receive the crown of life that the Lord has promised to those who love Him." (James 1:12, NIV)

Leadership in times of adversity reveals the strength and resilience of a leader. Trials are inevitable, but they also offer opportunities for growth, character development, and a deeper reliance on God. As leaders face challenges, their perseverance becomes a testimony of faith and trust in God's promises. In enduring hardship with a steadfast heart, leaders not only experience God's blessings but also inspire others to remain faithful during difficult seasons, knowing that God is faithful to fulfill His promises.

The Last Ash: How can you remain steadfast in leadership during challenging times?

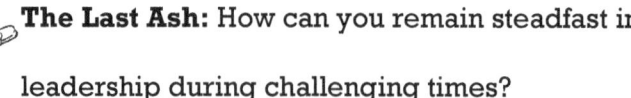

The Final Sip: How does trusting in God during trials shape your character and influence?

April 21

The Heart of Servanthood

"You, my brothers and sisters, were called to be free. But do not use your freedom to indulge the flesh; rather, serve one another humbly in love." (Galatians 5:13, NIV)

True servanthood is rooted in love, not obligation. As followers of Christ, we are called to use our freedom, not for selfish gain, but to serve others with humility and grace. The heart of servanthood is not about seeking recognition but about reflecting the love of Christ through our actions. By serving others selflessly, we fulfill God's command to love one another, demonstrating the transformative power of His love in our lives.

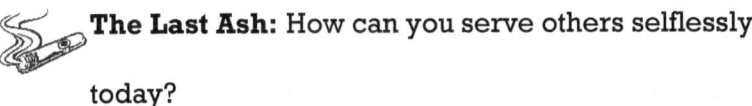 **The Last Ash:** How can you serve others selflessly today?

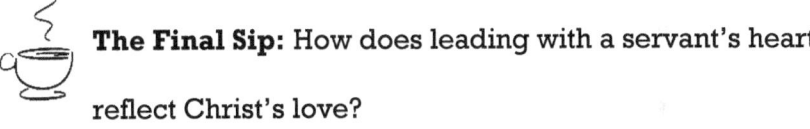 **The Final Sip:** How does leading with a servant's heart reflect Christ's love?

April 22

Speaking Truth in Love

"Instead, speaking the truth in love, we will grow to become in every respect the mature body of Him who is the head, that is, Christ." (Ephesians 4:15, NIV)

Speaking truth in love requires both courage and compassion. It's not enough to speak the truth; it must be delivered with kindness, respect, and a heart that seeks to build up rather than tear down. By balancing truth and love, we can foster growth in others while maintaining the unity of the body of Christ. Speaking the truth in love helps us to model Christ's character and to lead others toward spiritual maturity and deeper relationships with God.

The Last Ash: Where do you need to balance truth with love in your conversations?

The Final Sip: How does speaking truth with love build stronger, God-honoring relationships?

April 23

Leading by Example

"Don't let anyone look down on you because you are young, but set an example for the believers in speech, in conduct, in love, in faith, and in purity." (1 Timothy 4:12, NIV)

Leadership is not just about authority, but about setting a godly example in every area of life. Paul challenges Timothy, and by extension all believers, to lead by example, showing that integrity in our actions speaks louder than words. True leadership is demonstrated by living out Christ's teachings in our everyday conduct—our speech, our actions, and our attitudes. By exemplifying Christ-like behavior, we inspire others to follow and grow in their faith, regardless of age or position.

 The Last Ash: How can your actions today reflect Christ's example?

The Final Sip: How does living out your faith inspire those around you?

April 24

Listen Before You Speak

"Fools find no pleasure in understanding but delight in airing their own opinions." (Proverbs 18:2, NIV)

A fool focuses only on expressing their own thoughts, without considering others' perspectives or wisdom. For men striving to lead with integrity and influence, this verse is a reminder to pause, listen, and seek knowledge before speaking. Wisdom grows through humility and understanding, not through dominating conversations. When we choose to listen first, we build stronger relationships and gain insight that helps us respond with grace and wisdom.

The Last Ash: How can you listen with more intention in your conversations?

The Final Sip: When was the last time you learned something valuable by seeking to understand before speaking?

April 25

Finding Strength in God's Presence

"So do not fear, for I am with you; do not be dismayed, for I am your God. I will strengthen you and help you; I will uphold you with my righteous right hand." (Isaiah 41:10, NIV)

In times of fear and uncertainty, God promises to be our source of strength and security. Isaiah 41:10 reminds us that God's presence is not just a passive assurance but an active source of help in our lives. When we face challenges, we can find courage and confidence in the truth that God is with us, providing the strength we need to overcome any obstacle. Trusting in His presence allows us to face difficulties without fear, knowing that His power is more than enough to carry us through.

The Last Ash: Where do you need God's strength in your life right now?

The Final Sip: How does God's presence give you courage and confidence in leadership?

April 26

Leading with Compassion

"Therefore, as God's chosen people, holy and dearly loved, clothe yourselves with compassion, kindness, humility, gentleness, and patience." (Colossians 3:12, NIV)

Compassion is a foundational quality for leadership, especially for those following Christ. As leaders, we are called to embody the compassion that Jesus showed to others, offering kindness and understanding in the face of challenges. Colossians 3:12 teaches us that true leadership isn't about authority or power but about the willingness to serve others with gentleness and patience. By leading with compassion, we build trust and create an environment where others feel valued, cared for, and supported.

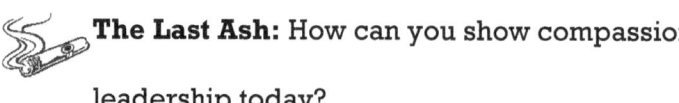 **The Last Ash:** How can you show compassion in your leadership today?

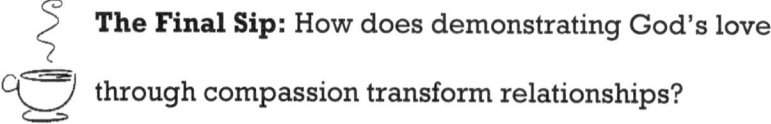 **The Final Sip:** How does demonstrating God's love through compassion transform relationships?

April 27

The Dangers of Pride in Leadership

"Pride goes before destruction, a haughty spirit before a fall." (Proverbs 16:18, NIV)

Pride is a destructive force, especially in leadership. Proverbs 16:18 reminds us that when leaders become proud and self-reliant, they are setting themselves up for failure. Pride blinds leaders to their own limitations and weaknesses, often causing them to make decisions that are not rooted in humility or wisdom. The antidote to pride is humility—recognizing that our strength comes from God and leading with a servant heart. A humble leader invites collaboration, listens to others, and remains open to correction, leading to better outcomes and greater influence.

The Last Ash: How can you guard against pride in your leadership today?

The Final Sip: How does humility enhance your leadership and decision-making?

April 28

Seeking Wisdom

"If any of you lacks wisdom, let him ask of God, who gives to all liberally and without reproach, and it will be given to him." (James 1:5, NIV)

Seeking wisdom is essential for effective leadership. James 1:5 offers a beautiful promise that God generously gives wisdom to those who ask. Wisdom isn't something we can manufacture on our own, but it is a gift from God that helps us navigate life's challenges with clarity and discernment. When leaders seek God's wisdom through prayer, reflection, and listening to His Word, they make decisions that honor God and lead others in the right direction.

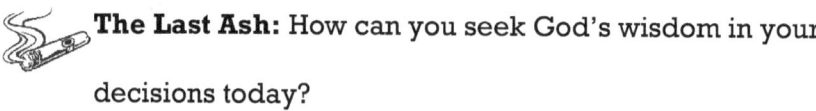**The Last Ash:** How can you seek God's wisdom in your decisions today?

The Final Sip: How does God's wisdom guide your leadership?

April 29

Persevering in the Race

"Therefore, since we are surrounded by such a great cloud of witnesses, let us throw off everything that hinders and the sin that so easily entangles. And let us run with perseverance the race marked out for us." (Hebrews 12:1, NIV)

Life and leadership are a race, requiring perseverance and endurance. Hebrews 12:1 encourages us to focus on the goal ahead, shedding anything that might distract or weigh us down. By fixing our eyes on Jesus, we can run the race with patience and persistence, trusting that He will equip us for the challenges we face. When we persevere, we honor God and inspire others to keep going, no matter how difficult the journey may be.

The Last Ash: What distractions or burdens do you need to cast off to persevere in your leadership?

The Final Sip: How does perseverance in faith and leadership reflect God's strength and faithfulness?

April 30

Trust and Take Action

"Trust in the Lord and do good; dwell in the land and enjoy safe pasture." (Psalm 37:3, NIV)

Trusting God means relying on His timing and provision, even when life feels uncertain. But this trust isn't passive. We're called to take action by doing good, making a positive impact on those around us. For men, this verse is a reminder to lead with integrity, make wise choices, and trust that God will provide a secure foundation for the future as we walk in obedience.

 The Last Ash: How can you show greater trust in God?

 **The Final Sip:** What good work can you do today to be a blessing to someone else?

May

Overcoming Adversity

This month highlights the examples of the turbulent world we live in and how we respond under duress.

Know you are capable.

May 1

Finding God's Purpose in Pain

"And we know that in all things God works for the good of those who love him, who have been called according to his purpose." (Romans 8:28, NIV)

While suffering is never easy, God uses it to shape us, refine our character, and ultimately fulfill His purpose in our lives. This truth brings comfort, knowing that even in the toughest times, God's plan is unfolding for our good and His glory.

The Last Ash: How can you find purpose in your current struggles?

The Final Sip: How does recognizing God's plan in your pain provide comfort and strength?

May 2

Strength through Surrender

"Submit yourselves, then, to God. Resist the devil, and he will flee from you." (James 4:7, NIV)

Submission isn't about weakness—it's about yielding our lives to God's authority and trusting His plan. At the same time, we are commanded to stand firm against temptation and the enemy's schemes. When we fully commit to God, we're equipped with His power to resist evil. For men, this verse is a call to be both humble and bold—surrendering to God's will while standing strong against anything that pulls us away from Him.

 **The Last Ash:** What areas of your life do you need to fully submit to God's authority?

The Final Sip: How can you stand firm and resist temptation more effectively?

May 3

God's Steady Hand

"For I am the Lord your God who takes hold of your right hand and says to you, 'Do not fear; I will help you.'"

(Isaiah 41:13, NIV)

God doesn't just send help from a distance—He takes us by the hand and walks with us through our struggles. It offers both comfort and strength. God's promise to help and protect us means we don't have to face fear or uncertainty alone. When we trust in His steady hand, we can move forward with confidence, knowing that He is always by our side.

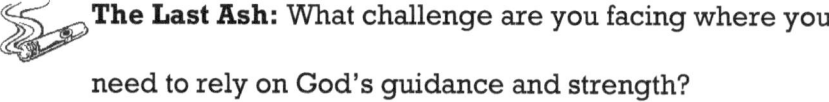**The Last Ash:** What challenge are you facing where you need to rely on God's guidance and strength?

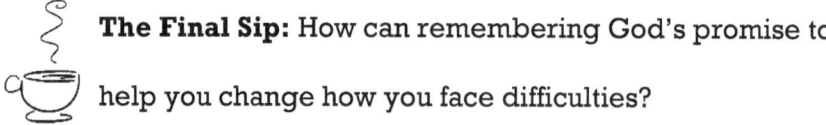**The Final Sip:** How can remembering God's promise to help you change how you face difficulties?

May 4

Strength in the Struggle

"I can do all this through him who gives me strength."

(Philippians 4:13, NIV)

In our own abilities, we may feel weak, but with Christ's strength, we are able to overcome obstacles and accomplish what seems impossible. It reminds us that we are not alone in our struggles and that our power comes from a source far greater than ourselves.

 The Last Ash: Where do you need to rely on Christ's strength to overcome a struggle today?

 **The Final Sip:** How does the strength Christ provides empower you to face challenges?

May 5

Trusting God's Timing

"He has made everything beautiful in its time. He has also set eternity in the human heart; yet no one can fathom what God has done from beginning to end." (Ecclesiastes 3:11, NIV)

God's timing is often different from our own, and we may not always understand why things happen when they do. This verse encourages us to trust that God's plan is perfect, even when we can't see the full picture. He orchestrates events with a purpose and in a time that is ultimately for our good. Patience and trust are essential as we wait on His timing.

The Last Ash: How can you trust in God's perfect timing during moments of waiting?

The Final Sip: How does trusting in God's timing reduce worry and foster peace?

May 6

Hope in the Midst of Despair

"The Lord is close to the brokenhearted and saves those who are crushed in spirit." (Psalm 34:18, NIV)

This scripture provides great comfort during times of grief and loss. When we are hurting and feel broken, God's presence is especially near, offering healing and solace. It is a reminder that God does not abandon us in our pain; He draws near to comfort and restore us.

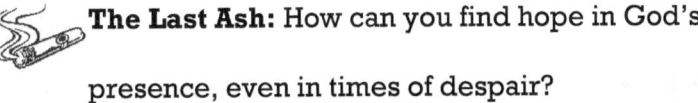**The Last Ash:** How can you find hope in God's presence, even in times of despair?

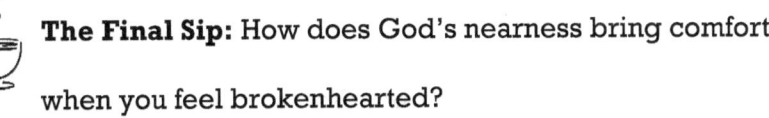**The Final Sip:** How does God's nearness bring comfort when you feel brokenhearted?

May 7

When You Feel Alone

"Be strong and courageous. Do not be afraid or terrified because of them, for the Lord your God goes with you; he will never leave you nor forsake you." (Deuteronomy 31:6, NIV)

Loneliness can be one of the most difficult emotions to face, but this verse assures us that we are never truly alone. God's presence is constant and unwavering. Even in the most solitary moments, He is with us, providing strength, courage, and comfort. We can face life's challenges with confidence because of His faithfulness.

**The Last Ash:** How can you remind yourself of God's constant presence when you feel isolated?

The Final Sip: How does God's promise never to leave you bring peace in moments of loneliness?

May 8

Persevering Through Trials

"No discipline seems pleasant at the time, but painful. Later on, however, it produces a harvest of righteousness and peace for those who have been trained by it." (Hebrews 12:11, NIV)

This passage teaches us that trials are not only inevitable, but they also serve a purpose in our lives. They develop perseverance, which strengthens our character and builds hope. While suffering is difficult, it is not in vain, as it deepens our trust in God and strengthens our faith in His promises.

The Last Ash: What trials are you currently facing, and how can you persevere with hope?

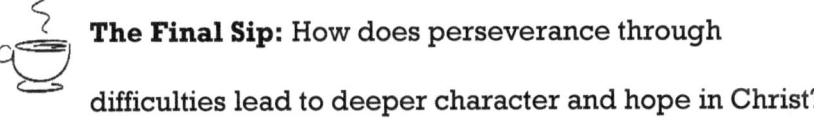

The Final Sip: How does perseverance through difficulties lead to deeper character and hope in Christ?

May 9

Overcoming Guilt with Grace

"If we confess our sins, he is faithful and just and will forgive us our sins and purify us from all unrighteousness."
(1 John 1:9, NIV)

Guilt can weigh heavily on our hearts, but this verse reminds us that we can find freedom and forgiveness in God. When we confess our sins, He is faithful to forgive and purify us, no matter how many times we fall short. God's grace is greater than our guilt, offering us a fresh start and a restored relationship with Him.

 **The Last Ash:** Where do you need to receive God's grace to overcome guilt in your life?

The Final Sip: How does confessing and receiving grace restore your relationship with God?

May 10

Turning Setbacks Into Comebacks

"Do not gloat over me, my enemy! Though I have fallen, I will rise. Though I sit in darkness, the Lord will be my light."

(Micah 7:8, NIV)

This scripture offers hope in the midst of defeat. Even when we face setbacks or failures, God's restorative power can lift us up and help us bounce back stronger. Rather than allowing our struggles to define us, we can trust that God is at work, turning our setbacks into opportunities for growth and comeback.

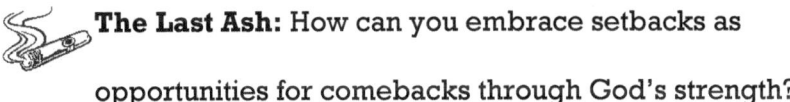**The Last Ash:** How can you embrace setbacks as opportunities for comebacks through God's strength?

**The Final Sip:** How does trusting in God's ability to redeem setbacks renew your hope for the future?

May 11

Defeating Doubt

"Immediately the boy's father exclaimed, "I do believe; help me overcome my unbelief!" (Mark 9:24, NIV)

Doubt is a common human experience, but this verse shows that even when we struggle with belief, we can turn to Jesus for help. The father's honest plea illustrates that faith is a journey, and Jesus is willing to help us overcome our doubts. This verse encourages us to acknowledge our doubts and seek God's help in building stronger faith.

The Last Ash: How can you overcome doubt and strengthen your faith in God's promises?

The Final Sip: How does acknowledging your doubts and trusting God lead to spiritual growth?

May 12

Trusting God in Uncertainty

"In their hearts humans plan their course, but the Lord establishes their steps." (Proverbs 16:9, NIV)

Life often takes unexpected turns, and uncertainty can leave us feeling uneasy. However, this verse assures us that God is in control, even when our plans don't unfold as expected. Trusting God's sovereignty and guidance in uncertain times gives us peace and confidence, knowing that He is ultimately directing our paths.

The Last Ash: How can you trust God's plan when you cannot see the outcome clearly?

The Final Sip: How does surrendering your uncertainty to God bring peace and direction?

May 13

Rejoicing in Suffering

"Dear friends, do not be surprised at the fiery ordeal that has come on you to test you, as though something strange were happening to you. But rejoice in as much as you participate in the sufferings of Christ, so that you may be overjoyed when his glory is revealed." (1 Peter 4:12-13, NIV)

Suffering is an inevitable part of the Christian walk, but this verse challenges us to change our perspective. Instead of seeing suffering as something to avoid, we are called to rejoice because it refines our faith and brings honor to God. Through our trials, we are drawn closer to Christ and our faith is made stronger.

The Last Ash: How can you rejoice in suffering, knowing that it refines your faith?

The Final Sip: How does rejoicing in suffering deepen your connection to Christ's suffering?

May 14

Surrendering Control to God

"But seek first his kingdom and his righteousness, and all these things will be given to you as well." (Matthew 6:33, NIV)

This verse calls us to prioritize God above everything else, trusting that He will take care of our needs. When we surrender control and focus on His will, we can experience peace, knowing that He will provide for us in ways we can't always foresee. Trusting in God's provision frees us from the anxiety of trying to control every detail of our lives.

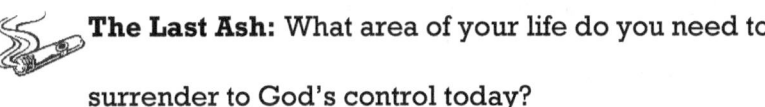**The Last Ash:** What area of your life do you need to surrender to God's control today?

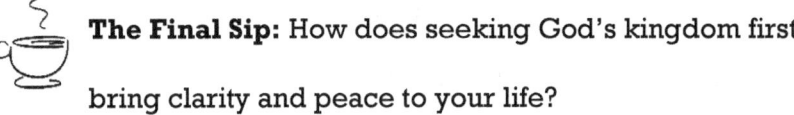**The Final Sip:** How does seeking God's kingdom first bring clarity and peace to your life?

May 15

Joy in God's Presence

"You make known to me the path of life; you will fill me with joy in your presence, with eternal pleasures at your right hand." (Psalm 16:11, NIV)

God's presence is a source of deep joy. This verse reminds us that when we draw near to God, He reveals the path of life and fills us with joy that transcends circumstances. The joy found in God's presence is eternal and unshakable, and it offers us peace that surpasses all understanding.

The Last Ash: How can you cultivate joy in God's presence today?

The Final Sip: How does seeking God's presence fill your heart with joy and peace?

May 15

Purpose in the Frustration

"For the creation was subjected to frustration, not by its own choice, but by the will of the one who subjected it, in hope." (Romans 8:20, NIV)

Frustration and hardship are inevitable, but they serve a purpose: to make us long for something greater and to trust in God's promise of renewal. For men who face life's challenges, this verse offers assurance that God is working even through the frustrations. There is hope beyond the struggle, and every difficulty is an opportunity to draw closer to Him and His purpose.

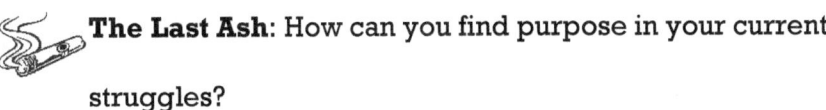**The Last Ash**: How can you find purpose in your current struggles?

**The Final Sip**: What has God taught you through difficult seasons that prepared you for future growth?

May 16

Living in Freedom

"Because through Christ Jesus the law of the Spirit who gives life has set you free from the law of sin and death."
(Romans 8:2, NIV)

Through His sacrifice, we are no longer bound by the power of sin and death but are given new life through the Spirit. This freedom isn't just about being forgiven; it's about living a life empowered by the Spirit to walk in victory and purpose. For men seeking to break free from destructive habits or burdens, this verse is a reminder that true freedom comes only through Christ. He offers the strength and grace to live in the fullness of His life-giving power.

The Last Ash: What areas of your life do you need to fully embrace the freedom Christ offers?

The Final Sip: How can living in the Spirit help you overcome struggles and walk in victory?

May 17

Patience in the Process

"Consider it pure joy, my brothers and sisters, whenever you face trials of many kinds, because you know that the testing of your faith produces perseverance. Let perseverance finish its work so that you may be mature and complete, not lacking anything." (James 1:2-4, NIV)

Patience is often seen as a virtue, but in this scripture, it is elevated to a key aspect of spiritual growth. Trials, although difficult, are seen as opportunities for growth. Rather than avoiding hardship, believers are called to embrace the process, knowing that God uses these experiences to build resilience and strengthen their faith. Over time, this perseverance leads to greater spiritual maturity and wholeness in Christ.

The Last Ash: What area of your life requires more patience during its process?

The Final Sip: How does patience in adversity build endurance and deepen your faith?

May 18

Facing Your Fears with Faith

"So do not fear, for I am with you; do not be dismayed, for I am your God. I will strengthen you and help you; I will uphold you with my righteous right hand." (Isaiah 41:10, NIV)

Fear can be overwhelming, but this verse reminds us that we are never alone. God's promise to be with us gives us the courage to face whatever challenges come our way. His presence provides strength, guidance, and comfort, turning our fears into opportunities for faith. When we rely on God's promises, we can overcome any fear, knowing that He is our constant support.

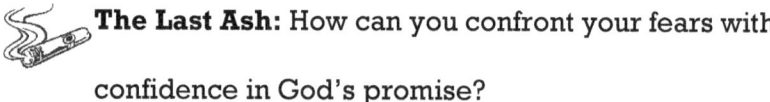**The Last Ash:** How can you confront your fears with confidence in God's promise?

**The Final Sip:** How does faith transform fear and lead you to courage in tough times?

May 19

The Power of Wise Instruction

"Hold on to instruction, do not let it go; guard it well, for it is your life." (Proverbs 4:13, NIV)

It's not enough to hear wisdom—we must embrace it, protect it, and apply it to our decisions. For men seeking to live with purpose and integrity, this verse is a call to value wise counsel and biblical truth, treating it as essential to life and success. God's instruction is not a burden but a source of protection and guidance that keeps us on the right path.

The Last Ash: How can you be more intentional about applying godly wisdom in your daily decisions?

The Final Sip: What practical steps can you take to guard and protect the instruction you've received from God's Word?

May 20

Trusting God's Timing

"He has made everything beautiful in its time. He has also set eternity in the human heart; yet no one can fathom what God has done from beginning to end." (Ecclesiastes 3:11, NIV)

This verse speaks to the importance of trusting God's timing, especially when life doesn't unfold as we expect. While we may desire immediate answers or outcomes, God's perfect timing is always for our good and His glory. Understanding that He is sovereign over time allows believers to rest in His plan, even in periods of waiting or uncertainty, knowing that everything will happen at the right moment according to His will.

**The Last Ash:** How can you trust in God's perfect timing during moments of waiting?

The Final Sip: How does trusting in God's timing reduce worry and foster peace?

May 21

God's Faithfulness in Trouble

"The righteous person may have many troubles, but the Lord delivers him from them all." (Psalm 34:19, NIV)

Troubles may be part of life, but they don't define our story. For men facing difficulties, this verse offers hope and assurance that God is present in every hardship. His deliverance may not always come how or when we expect, but it's always perfect. Trusting in His faithfulness gives us the strength to persevere and remain confident in His care.

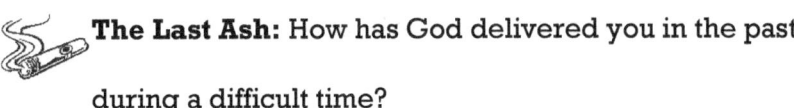**The Last Ash:** How has God delivered you in the past during a difficult time?

**The Final Sip:** How can trusting God's promise of deliverance give you peace in your current struggles?

May 22

God Goes Before You

"The Lord himself goes before you and will be with you; he will never leave you nor forsake you. Do not be afraid; do not be discouraged." (Deuteronomy 31:8, NIV)

As Moses speaks to Joshua and the people of Israel, he reminds them that they are not stepping into the unknown alone—God is already there, leading the way. For men facing uncertainty or challenges, this verse is a source of strength and comfort. God's assurance that He will never leave or forsake us means we can move forward with courage and confidence, knowing that we are never abandoned or without direction.

**The Last Ash:** What area of your life do you need to trust that God is going before you?

The Final Sip: How does knowing God will never leave or forsake you change how you face fear or uncertainty?

May 23

Persevering Through Trials

"Not only so, but we also glory in our sufferings, because we know that suffering produces perseverance; perseverance, character; and character, hope. And hope does not put us to shame, because God's love has been poured out into our hearts through the Holy Spirit, who has been given to us."
(Romans 5:3-5, NIV)

This scripture highlights the transformative power of trials. Though difficult, suffering can be an opportunity for growth and spiritual development. Through perseverance, we develop deeper character and an enduring hope that is anchored in God's faithfulness. As we face challenges, we can trust that God uses them to shape us into more resilient and hopeful individuals, drawing us closer to Him in the process.

The Last Ash: What trials are you currently facing, and how can you persevere with hope?

The Final Sip: How does perseverance through difficulties lead to deeper character and hope in Christ?

May 24

Honesty Before God

"If we claim we have not sinned, we make him out to be a liar and his word is not in us." (1 John 1:10, NIV)

Denying our sin not only distances us from God but also rejects His truth and grace. For men striving to grow spiritually and lead well, this verse calls for self-reflection and an honest acknowledgment of our weaknesses. Owning our failures doesn't lead to condemnation—it opens the door for forgiveness, healing, and deeper connection with God. True strength begins with being real before Him.

The Last Ash: Why is it important to acknowledge your sins before God?

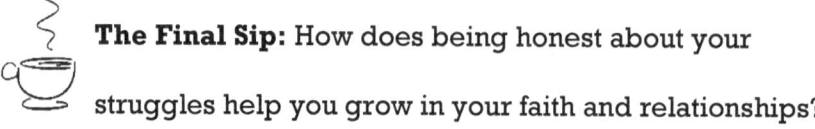

The Final Sip: How does being honest about your struggles help you grow in your faith and relationships?

May 25

Turning Setbacks Into Comebacks

"But as for me, I watch in hope for the Lord, I wait for God my Savior; my God will hear me." (Micah 7:7, NIV)

Micah chooses to focus on hope and patience, confident that God will respond. Waiting on God is not passive—it's an active stance of faith and expectation, knowing that He hears and answers in His perfect timing. When we watch and wait with hope, we find strength and peace in God's promises.

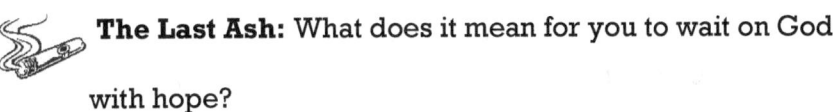

The Last Ash: What does it mean for you to wait on God with hope?

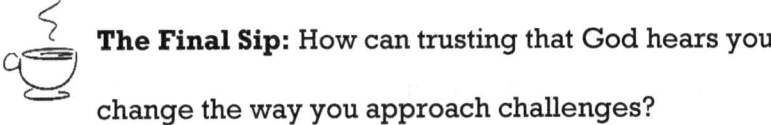

The Final Sip: How can trusting that God hears you change the way you approach challenges?

May 26

The Lifting Hand of Jesus

"But Jesus took him by the hand and lifted him to his feet, and he stood up." (Mark 9:27, NIV)

After healing a boy oppressed by an evil spirit, Jesus extends His hand and lifts him up. This verse reminds us that Jesus not only delivers us from our struggles but also helps us stand again. For men facing setbacks or hardships, this is a powerful image of hope—Jesus is always ready to reach out, steady us, and help us rise. We are never too far down for His hand to lift us back up.

The Last Ash: In what area of your life do you need to take hold of Jesus' hand and let Him lift you?

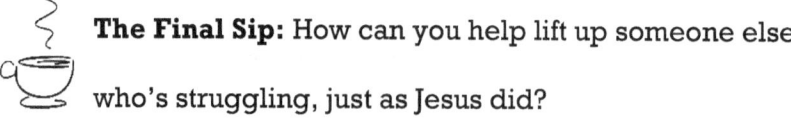

The Final Sip: How can you help lift up someone else who's struggling, just as Jesus did?

May 27

The Value of Honesty

"Kings take pleasure in honest lips; they value the one who speaks what is right." (Proverbs 16:13, NIV)

Those who speak truth and stand for what is right earn respect and trust. For men called to lead and influence others, this verse is a reminder that our words matter. Honesty isn't always easy, but it builds credibility and reflects God's character. Speaking what is right—especially in challenging situations—brings honor to God and strengthens the people around us.

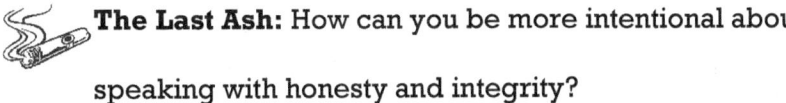**The Last Ash:** How can you be more intentional about speaking with honesty and integrity?

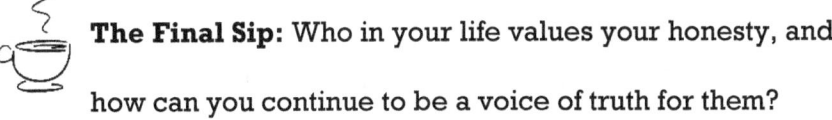**The Final Sip:** Who in your life values your honesty, and how can you continue to be a voice of truth for them?

May 28

Blessed in the Struggle

"If you are insulted because of the name of Christ, you are blessed, for the Spirit of glory and of God rests on you."
(1 Peter 4:14, NIV)

It reminds us that being insulted for following Christ isn't a sign of failure—it's a mark of blessing. God's Spirit is present in those moments, giving strength and reassurance. For men striving to stand firm in their faith, this verse is a call to embrace challenges with confidence, knowing that God is with us. His Spirit rests on us, providing the power to endure and remain steadfast.

The Last Ash: How can you remain confident and faithful when facing criticism or opposition for your beliefs?

The Final Sip: What does it mean to you that God's Spirit rests on you in moments of struggle?

May 29

Trusting God's Provision

"Look at the birds of the air; they do not sow or reap or store away in barns, and yet your heavenly Father feeds them. Are you not much more valuable than they?" (Matthew 6:26, NIV)

If He takes care of the birds—creatures with no means of planning or storing—how much more will He care for us? This verse challenges us to let go of anxiety and trust that God knows our needs and will provide in His perfect timing. For men balancing responsibilities and concerns about the future, it's a call to rest in the assurance that our value to God far exceeds anything we can imagine. Trusting Him allows us to live with peace and confidence.

The Last Ash: What area of your life do you need to trust God's provision more fully?

The Final Sip: How does knowing your value to God change the way you approach your daily concerns?

May 30

Victory Through Christ

"But thanks be to God! He gives us the victory through our Lord Jesus Christ." (1 Corinthians 15:57, NIV)

This verse celebrates the ultimate victory that believers have through Christ. His death and resurrection have secured victory over sin and death, and as a result, we can live in the freedom He provides. This victory is not just for the future, but it impacts our daily lives, enabling us to overcome challenges and walk in newness of life. Our response is one of gratitude, as we recognize that all victory comes through Christ alone.

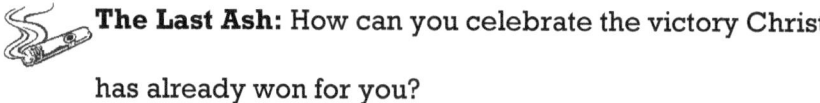**The Last Ash:** How can you celebrate the victory Christ has already won for you?

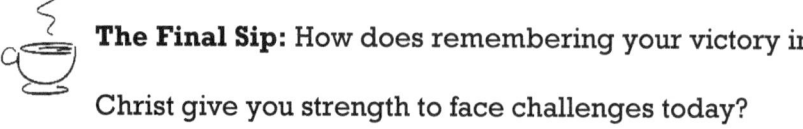**The Final Sip:** How does remembering your victory in Christ give you strength to face challenges today?

May 31

Walking in God's Peace

"Do not be anxious about anything, but in every situation, by prayer and petition, with thanksgiving, present your requests to God. And the peace of God, which transcends all understanding, will guard your hearts and your minds in Christ Jesus." (Philippians 4:6-7, NIV)

In times of stress and anxiety, this scripture offers a powerful promise. When we bring our concerns to God in prayer, we are given a peace that transcends understanding. This peace doesn't come from circumstances, but from God Himself, guarding our hearts and minds in Christ Jesus. By trusting God with our worries, we experience His peace, which empowers us to face life's challenges with calm and assurance.

 **The Last Ash:** How can you surrender your anxieties to God and experience His peace today?

The Final Sip: How does God's peace guard your heart and mind in times of stress or uncertainty?

June

Strength for Daily Living

In June, let's focus on a routine.

It's not only how you start, it's how you finish.

June 1

The Power of Morning Devotions

"In the morning, Lord, you hear my voice; in the morning I lay my requests before you and wait expectantly." (Psalm 5:3, NIV)

Starting the day with prayer and devotion sets the tone for everything that follows. Psalm 5:3 reminds us that God listens to our prayers, and when we seek Him in the morning, we align our hearts with His will. Morning devotions provide a time of renewal, allowing us to surrender our plans to Him and face the day with faith and expectancy.

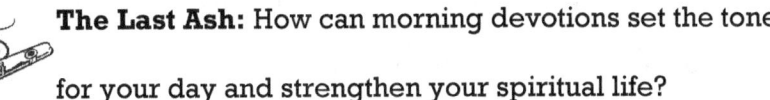 **The Last Ash:** How can morning devotions set the tone for your day and strengthen your spiritual life?

 **The Final Sip:** How does beginning your day in prayer and scripture bring peace and clarity?

June 2

Staying Spiritually Fit

"For physical training is of some value, but godliness has value for all things, holding promise for both the present life and the life to come." (1 Timothy 4:8, NIV)

Just as physical exercise strengthens the body, spiritual disciplines—such as prayer, Bible study, and worship—strengthen our faith. Paul emphasizes that while physical training is beneficial, cultivating godliness has eternal rewards. Staying spiritually fit means consistently growing in our relationship with God and living in obedience to His Word.

**The Last Ash:** What spiritual practices can you commit to for maintaining spiritual health?

The Final Sip: How does staying spiritually fit enable you to grow in godliness and handle life's challenges?

June 3

Living in the Present Moment

"Therefore do not worry about tomorrow, for tomorrow will worry about itself. Each day has enough trouble of its own." (Matthew 6:34, NIV)

Jesus teaches us to focus on today rather than be consumed with anxiety about the future. Worry robs us of peace and joy, but trusting in God's provision allows us to live fully in the present. By embracing each moment with faith, we experience His blessings and find contentment in the here and now.

 **The Last Ash:** How can focusing on the present moment help you trust God more fully?

The Final Sip: How does embracing today and letting go of worries for tomorrow lead to peace?

June 4

Choosing Joy Every Day

"Rejoice in the Lord always. I will say it again: Rejoice!" (Philippians 4:4, NIV)

Paul encourages believers to choose joy, regardless of circumstances. True joy is found in God, not in external situations. By focusing on His goodness and faithfulness, we can maintain a heart of gratitude and positivity, even during difficult times. Joy is a daily decision to trust in His sovereignty.

 **The Last Ash:** How can you make the choice to rejoice in God's goodness today?

The Final Sip: How does choosing joy each day help you maintain a positive perspective, no matter your circumstances?

June 5

Faithful in Prayer, Strong in Hope

"Be joyful in hope, patient in affliction, faithful in prayer." (Romans 12:12, NIV)

Prayer keeps us connected to His strength and aligns our hearts with His will. Being faithful in prayer doesn't mean praying only when things get tough—it's about cultivating a consistent habit of turning to God in every situation. When we remain joyful in hope, patient in trials, and persistent in prayer, we develop the resilience needed to lead well and stay the course.

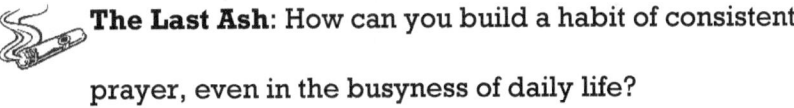 **The Last Ash**: How can you build a habit of consistent prayer, even in the busyness of daily life?

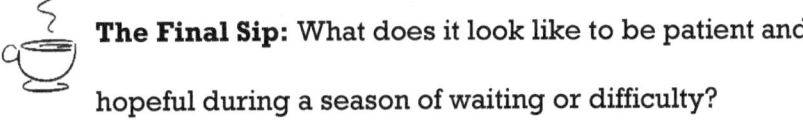 **The Final Sip:** What does it look like to be patient and hopeful during a season of waiting or difficulty?

June 6

Overcoming Busyness with Balance

"Martha, Martha," the Lord answered, "you are worried and upset about many things, but few things are needed—or indeed only one. Mary has chosen what is better, and it will not be taken away from her." (Luke 10:41-42, NIV)

Jesus reminds Martha that while serving is important, spending time with Him is even more valuable. In our busy lives, it's easy to get distracted by responsibilities, but prioritizing our relationship with Christ brings true fulfillment. Finding balance means making time for God amid our daily tasks.

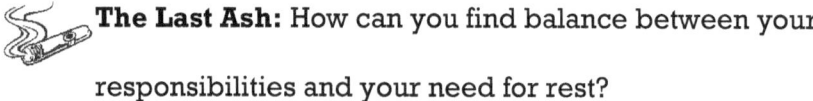**The Last Ash:** How can you find balance between your responsibilities and your need for rest?

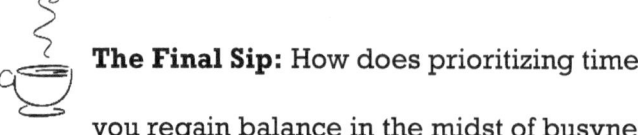**The Final Sip:** How does prioritizing time with God help you regain balance in the midst of busyness?

June 7

Restoring Your Soul Through Sabbath

"Remember the Sabbath day by keeping it holy. Six days you shall labor and do all your work, but the seventh day is a Sabbath to the Lord your God." (Exodus 20:8-10, NIV)

God established the Sabbath as a day of rest and renewal. Taking time to pause, reflect, and worship allows us to recharge spiritually and physically. When we honor the Sabbath, we acknowledge our dependence on God and create space for Him to restore our souls.

**The Last Ash**: How can observing a Sabbath rest restore your soul and refresh your spirit?

The Final Sip: How does intentionally setting aside time for rest deepen your relationship with God?

June 8

Gratitude as a Daily Habit

"Rejoice always, pray continually, give thanks in all circumstances; for this is God's will for you in Christ Jesus." (1 Thessalonians 5:16-18, NIV)

Gratitude shifts our focus from what we lack to the abundance of blessings God has given us. Developing a habit of thankfulness strengthens our faith and brings joy. Even in difficult situations, choosing gratitude allows us to experience God's presence and peace.

The Last Ash: How can cultivating a habit of gratitude impact your daily outlook?

The Final Sip: How does giving thanks in all circumstances foster a deeper connection with God?

June 9

Choosing Your Words Wisely

"The tongue has the power of life and death, and those who love it will eat its fruit." (Proverbs 18:21, NIV)

Our words have the ability to uplift or tear down, bless or harm. Proverbs reminds us to speak with wisdom and kindness. Choosing words that encourage and build others up reflects God's love and brings positive change in our relationships.

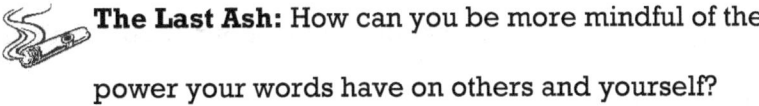 **The Last Ash:** How can you be more mindful of the power your words have on others and yourself?

 **The Final Sip:** How does choosing words that speak life rather than harm strengthen your relationships?

June 10

From Worry to Worship

"Therefore I tell you, do not worry about your life, what you will eat or drink; or about your body, what you will wear. Is not life more than food, and the body more than clothes? Look at the birds of the air; they do not sow or reap or store away in barns, and yet your heavenly Father feeds them. Are you not much more valuable than they?" (Matthew 6:25-27, NIV)

Jesus invites us to trust in God's provision instead of being consumed by worry. When we shift our focus from anxiety to worship, we acknowledge His sovereignty and faithfulness. Worshiping God reminds us that He cares for our needs and has a plan for our lives.

The Last Ash: How can you turn moments of worry into opportunities for worship and trust in God?

The Final Sip: How does worship redirect your focus from anxiety to God's provision and care?

June 11

Turning Small Moments Into Big Impacts

"His master replied, 'Well done, good and faithful servant! You have been faithful with a few things; I will put you in charge of many things. Come and share your master's happiness!'" (Matthew 25:21, NIV)

When we are diligent and faithful in the little things, God entrusts us with greater opportunities to serve and make a difference for His kingdom.

 **The Last Ash:** How can you turn ordinary moments into opportunities to serve God and others?

The Final Sip: How does faithfulness in the little things lead to greater responsibility and impact in God's kingdom?

June 12

Walking in the Spirit Daily

"So I say, walk by the Spirit, and you will not gratify the desires of the flesh." (Galatians 5:16, NIV)

Living by the Spirit means allowing God to guide our thoughts, actions, and decisions. When we walk in the Spirit, we resist sin and grow in Christ-like character. It's a daily commitment to align our lives with His will.

 **The Last Ash:** How can you walk in the Spirit daily and allow God's guidance in your decisions?

The Final Sip: How does living in the Spirit transform your actions, thoughts, and relationships?

June 13

Taking Every Thought Captive

"We demolish arguments and every pretension that sets itself up against the knowledge of God, and we take captive every thought to make it obedient to Christ." (2 Corinthians 10:5, NIV)

Our minds are a battlefield, but through Christ, we have the power to control our thoughts. By surrendering negative and harmful thoughts to Him, we can replace them with truth and wisdom. Renewing our minds leads to transformation.

The Last Ash: How can you actively take your thoughts captive and align them with Christ?

The Final Sip: How does controlling your thoughts lead to spiritual transformation and greater peace?

June 14

Aligning Your Plans with God's Will

"Many are the plans in a person's heart, but it is the Lord's purpose that prevails." (Proverbs 19:21, NIV)

While we make plans for our future, God's purpose ultimately prevails. Trusting Him means being open to His direction and allowing Him to guide our steps. Surrendering our plans to Him leads to a life of fulfillment and purpose.

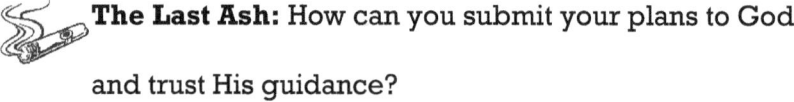 **The Last Ash:** How can you submit your plans to God and trust His guidance?

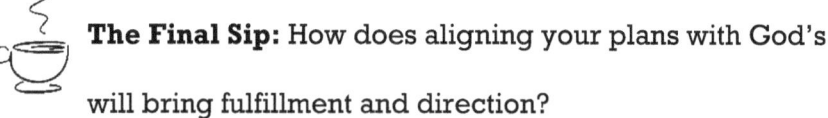 **The Final Sip:** How does aligning your plans with God's will bring fulfillment and direction?

June 15

Redeeming the Time

"Be very careful, then, how you live—not as unwise but as wise, making the most of every opportunity, because the days are evil." (Ephesians 5:15-16, NIV)

Time is a precious gift, and Paul urges us to use it wisely. Instead of being distracted or wasting time, we should seek opportunities to grow spiritually, serve others, and fulfill God's calling. Living intentionally allows us to make the most of every moment.

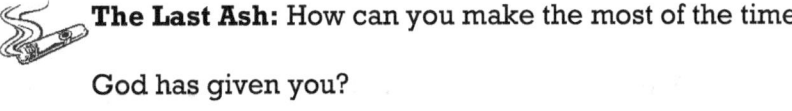**The Last Ash:** How can you make the most of the time God has given you?

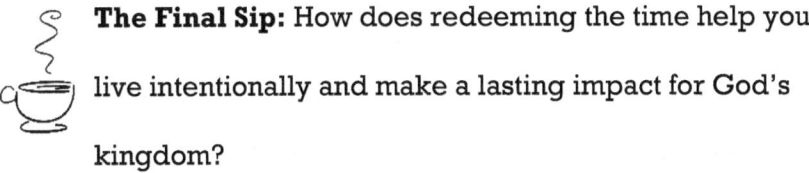**The Final Sip:** How does redeeming the time help you live intentionally and make a lasting impact for God's kingdom?

June 16

Living in Freedom

"So if the Son sets you free, you will be free indeed."

(John 8:36, NIV)

True freedom comes from Christ. Many people seek freedom in worldly pleasures, success, or self-sufficiency, but Jesus teaches that real freedom is found in Him. When we surrender our lives to Christ, we are released from the bondage of sin, fear, and guilt. Embracing God's freedom means walking confidently in His grace, knowing we are no longer enslaved to our past or the pressures of the world.

 **The Last Ash:** How does knowing that Christ has set you free empower you to live boldly?

The Final Sip: How can embracing God's freedom in your life bring peace and confidence?

June 17

Trusting in God's Provision

"And my God will meet all your needs according to the riches of his glory in Christ Jesus." (Philippians 4:19, NIV)

This verse reminds us that God is our ultimate provider. In times of uncertainty, financial strain, or personal need, we can trust that He will supply everything necessary for our well-being. However, His provision isn't always material—it includes peace, wisdom, and strength to endure challenges. Trusting in God's provision means relying on Him instead of worrying, knowing He cares for us and will never leave us lacking.

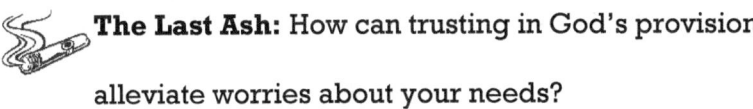 **The Last Ash:** How can trusting in God's provision alleviate worries about your needs?

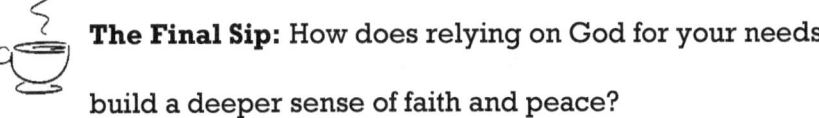 **The Final Sip:** How does relying on God for your needs build a deeper sense of faith and peace?

June 18

Living with Purpose

"For I know the plans I have for you," declares the Lord, "plans to prosper you and not to harm you, plans to give you hope and a future." (Jeremiah 29:11, NIV)

God has a divine purpose for each of us. Even in times of uncertainty or struggle, we can find comfort knowing that God's plans are good. Living with purpose means aligning our lives with His will, seeking His guidance, and trusting that every season—whether joyful or challenging—is leading us toward His greater plan. Our purpose isn't just about personal success but about fulfilling God's mission for our lives.

 **The Last Ash:** How can you align your life with the purpose God has designed for you?

The Final Sip: How does living with a sense of purpose bring fulfillment and direction?

June 19

Restoring Relationships

"All this is from God, who reconciled us to himself through Christ and gave us the ministry of reconciliation: that God was reconciling the world to himself in Christ, not counting people's sins against them." (2 Corinthians 5:18-19, NIV)

As believers, we are called to restore relationships, just as Christ restored our relationship with God. This includes forgiveness, humility, and seeking peace with others. Whether it's healing broken friendships, family tensions, or conflicts within the church, reconciliation reflects God's love. True restoration requires grace and a willingness to let go of past hurts, just as God does for us.

The Last Ash: How can you seek reconciliation in strained relationships and reflect God's love?

The Final Sip: How does restoring relationships bring healing and peace to both parties involved?

June 20

The Value of Godly Wisdom

"If any of you lacks wisdom, you should ask God, who gives generously to all without finding fault, and it will be given to you." (James 1:5, NIV)

Worldly wisdom is limited, but godly wisdom leads to clarity and truth. James reminds us that when we seek wisdom from God, He provides it generously. This means praying for guidance in decisions, relationships, and daily life. Instead of relying on human understanding, seeking God's wisdom helps us navigate life with discernment, peace, and confidence in His direction.

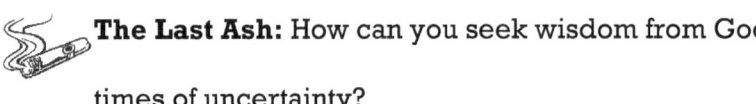**The Last Ash:** How can you seek wisdom from God in times of uncertainty?

The Final Sip: How does godly wisdom help guide your decisions and actions?

June 21

Power of Prayer

"Ask and it will be given to you; seek and you will find; knock and the door will be opened to you. For everyone who asks receives; the one who seeks finds; and to the one who knocks, the door will be opened." (Matthew 7:7-8, NIV)

Prayer is a powerful connection to God, and Jesus teaches us to pray with persistence and faith. When we seek God through prayer, He hears us and responds according to His will. This doesn't mean every request is answered as we expect, but that God is always working for our good. Praying in faith means trusting Him, even when we don't see immediate results.

The Last Ash: How can you approach God in prayer with boldness and faith?

The Final Sip: How does persistent prayer strengthen your relationship with God and bring answers?

June 22

Building Unshakable Faith

"Now faith is confidence in what we hope for and assurance about what we do not see." (Hebrews 11:1, NIV)

Faith isn't based on circumstances—it's trusting in God even when we can't see the outcome. Building unshakable faith means standing firm in God's promises, especially during trials. Like the heroes of faith in Hebrews 11, we must trust that God is working, even when we don't understand His plan. Strengthening our faith requires daily reliance on Him through prayer, Scripture, and obedience.

 **The Last Ash**: How can you strengthen your faith in God's promises despite doubts or challenges?

The Final Sip: How does unwavering faith in God lead to growth and transformation?

June 23

Walking in Integrity

"Whoever walks in integrity walks securely, but whoever takes crooked paths will be found out." (Proverbs 10:9, NIV)

Integrity means living honestly and righteously, even when no one is watching. Proverbs teaches that those who walk with integrity have nothing to fear, while deception eventually leads to downfall. Living with integrity builds trust, honors God, and ensures that our actions align with our beliefs.

The Last Ash: How can you walk with integrity in all areas of your life?

The Final Sip: How does living with integrity reflect your faith and bring honor to God?

June 24

The Joy of Generosity

"Each of you should give what you have decided in your heart to give, not reluctantly or under compulsion, for God loves a cheerful giver." (2 Corinthians 9:7, NIV)

Generosity isn't just about money—it's about a heart willing to bless others. Giving joyfully reflects God's own generosity toward us. Whether it's financial support, time, or encouragement, God calls us to give freely and with love. When we give with a cheerful heart, we experience the true joy of selflessness.

 **The Last Ash:** How does giving generously impact both the giver and the receiver?

The Final Sip: How does the act of giving reflect God's heart and bring blessings?

June 25

Faith Over Fear

"For the Spirit God gave us does not make us timid, but gives us power, love and self-discipline." (2 Timothy 1:7, NIV)

Fear can hold us back, but faith empowers us. God has given us a spirit of courage, not fear. When we rely on His strength, we can face challenges with confidence, knowing that He equips us with the power, love, and discipline needed to overcome obstacles.

 **The Last Ash:** How can faith in God help you overcome fear in difficult situations?

The Final Sip: How does trusting God in the face of fear bring peace and courage?

June 26

Loving Others as Christ Loves You

"A new command I give you: Love one another. As I have loved you, so you must love one another. By this everyone will know that you are my disciples, if you love one another."

(John 13:34-35, NIV)

Jesus calls us to love others selflessly and sacrificially. Our love should reflect His—unconditional, forgiving, and active. Loving others isn't just about feelings but actions that show Christ's love to the world.

 **The Last Ash:** How can you show Christ's love to others in practical ways?

The Final Sip: How does walking in love reflect your relationship with Christ and draw others to Him?

June 27

Unshakable Faith in Adversity

"Therefore put on the full armor of God, so that when the day of evil comes, you may be able to stand your ground, and after you have done everything, to stand." (Ephesians 6:13, NIV)

Faith is not just believing in God—it is standing firm in His truth, especially in difficult times. Paul encourages believers to equip themselves with the armor of God to withstand trials and spiritual attacks. This means staying rooted in Scripture, prayer, and righteousness. Standing firm in faith requires courage and reliance on God's strength rather than our own.

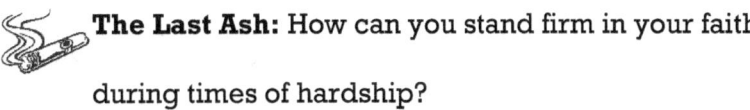**The Last Ash:** How can you stand firm in your faith during times of hardship?

**The Final Sip:** How does standing firm in God's promises bring strength and resilience?

June 28

The Power of Forgiveness

"Make every effort to keep the unity of the Spirit through the bond of peace." (Ephesians 4:3, NIV)

Unity doesn't happen by accident—it requires intentionality, humility, and perseverance. This verse reminds men to be peacemakers and bridge-builders, setting aside pride and selfishness for the sake of harmony. True strength is shown in fostering peace, promoting understanding, and working together for a greater purpose. When we live in unity, we reflect God's love and create stronger families, teams, and communities.

The Last Ash: How can you be a stronger example of unity and peace?

The Final Sip: What personal attitudes or behaviors might be hindering peace and unity in your life?

June 29

Grace That Transforms

"But he said to me, 'My grace is sufficient for you, for my power is made perfect in weakness.' Therefore I will boast all the more gladly about my weaknesses, so that Christ's power may rest on me." (2 Corinthians 12:9, NIV)

God's grace is more than enough for any challenge we face. Paul reminds us that our weaknesses allow God's power to shine through. Instead of being discouraged by our limitations, we can trust in His grace to sustain and transform us. Embracing grace means accepting God's love despite our flaws and allowing Him to work in our lives.

The Last Ash: How can you embrace God's grace in moments of weakness or failure?

The Final Sip: How does experiencing God's grace lead to transformation and greater dependence on Him?

June 30

Living with Eternal Perspective

"Since then you have been raised with Christ, set your hearts on things above, where Christ is, seated at the right hand of God. Set your minds on things above, not on earthly things."
(Colossians 3:1-2, NIV)

As believers, our focus should be on eternity rather than temporary worldly concerns. Living with an eternal perspective means prioritizing our relationship with God, investing in things that have lasting value, and trusting in His ultimate plan. When we keep our eyes on Christ, we find peace, purpose, and joy beyond what this world can offer.

The Last Ash: How can living with an eternal perspective help you navigate the challenges of this life?

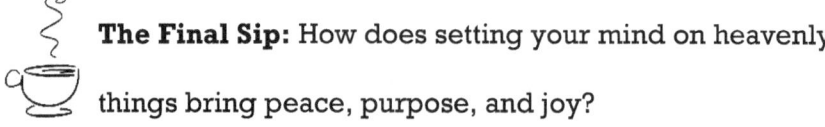

The Final Sip: How does setting your mind on heavenly things bring peace, purpose, and joy?

July

Faith and Identity

This month we hold firm knowing our identity is not of the world or the pressures we face, but from Christ alone.

July 1

Understanding Who You Are in Christ

"Therefore, if anyone is in Christ, the new creation has come: The old has gone, the new is here!" (2 Corinthians 5:17, NIV)

When we accept Christ, we are not merely improved versions of our old selves—we are completely transformed. Our past mistakes, failures, and identities no longer define us. Instead, we are made new through His grace. This transformation brings freedom from guilt and shame, allowing us to step forward with confidence into the life God has designed for us.

The Last Ash: How does recognizing your new identity in Christ transform your outlook on life?

The Final Sip: How does understanding you are a new creation in Christ empower you to live confidently?

July 2

Made in His Image: The Value of Every Man

"So God created mankind in his own image, in the image of God he created them; male and female he created them." (Genesis 1:27, NIV)

Our worth is not determined by our achievements, status, or the opinions of others—it is inherent because we are made in His likeness. Understanding this truth should transform how we see ourselves, replacing insecurity with confidence and purpose. It also challenges us to honor and respect others, recognizing that every human life reflects the divine Creator.

 **Last Ash:** How does knowing you are made in God's image affect how you view yourself and others?

The Final Sip: How can embracing the truth that all people are made in God's image change the way we treat one another?

July 3

God's Masterpiece: Walking in Your Purpose

"For we are God's handiwork, created in Christ Jesus to do good works, which God prepared in advance for us to do." (Ephesians 2:10, NIV)

As His masterpiece, we are designed with purpose, created to live out the good works He has already set before us. Embracing this truth means walking confidently in the calling He has placed on our lives, knowing that our talents, experiences, and even our struggles all serve a greater purpose. When we align our lives with God's plan, we find fulfillment, joy, and a deep sense of meaning.

**The Last Ash:** How can understanding you are God's workmanship guide you in fulfilling His purpose for your life?

The Final Sip: How does walking in your God-given purpose bring meaning and fulfillment to your daily life?

July 4

Freedom in Christ: Breaking the Chains

"It is for freedom that Christ has set us free. Stand firm, then, and do not let yourselves be burdened again by a yoke of slavery." (Galatians 5:1, NIV)

Paul's letter to the Galatians highlights the purpose of Christ's sacrifice: freedom. Christ didn't die to set us free only to have us return to a life of bondage—whether it be to sin, fear, or worldly concerns Embracing this freedom means recognizing that the chains of sin no longer control us, and that fear no longer has a hold on us. It's about walking confidently in the grace and liberty given to us through Christ, knowing we are no longer slaves to past habits, regrets, or uncertainties.

The Last Ash: Reflect on how Christ's sacrifice has liberated you from things that once held you down.

The Final Sip: How can this freedom fuel your courage to live authentically and boldly in all areas of your life?

July 5

Living as a Citizen of Heaven

"But our citizenship is in heaven. And we eagerly await a Savior from there, the Lord Jesus Christ." (Philippians 3:20, NIV)

As believers, our identity is not rooted in the temporary, earthly systems or cultures we belong to but in the eternal kingdom of heaven. Being citizens of heaven means living with a higher perspective—our values, priorities, and actions should reflect the principles of God's kingdom, not those of this world. We are not defined by earthly labels or temporary struggles, but by our relationship with Christ and our hope in His return.

The Last Ash: How do your values and actions align with your eternal home?

The Final Sip: In the midst of life's challenges and distractions, how can you keep the eternal in view, allowing it to guide your choices and attitudes as you go about your day?

July 6

Chosen and Loved by God

"But you are a chosen people, a royal priesthood, a holy nation, God's special possession, that you may declare the praises of him who called you out of darkness into his wonderful light." (1 Peter 2:9, NIV)

We are chosen by God, set apart as His royal priesthood, and considered His special possession. Our worth and value are not determined by the world's standards but by God's deliberate choice and unconditional love for us. It calls us to live with a sense of dignity, purpose, and honor, knowing that we are deeply loved and valued by the Creator of the universe.

The Last Ash: How does knowing you are chosen and loved by the Creator influence your confidence and how you interact with the world?

The Final Sip: How can this realization inspire you to step into your calling with boldness and live out your purpose today?

July 7

Boldly Approaching the Throne of Grace

"Let us then approach God's throne of grace with confidence, so that we may receive mercy and find grace to help us in our time of need." (Hebrews 4:16, NIV)

This verse invites believers to approach God's throne of grace not with hesitation or fear, but with confidence. Through Jesus, we have been granted direct access to God, and He welcomes us with open arms. This invitation is not just for moments of joy but especially for times of need, when we are struggling or seeking help.

The Last Ash: Do you approach God with confidence, or do you hold back?

The Final Sip: Confidence in God's grace and mercy frees us from the fear of approaching Him. How does this confidence empower you to approach God in your daily life?

July 8

From Sinner to Saint: Embracing Your New Identity

"Therefore, there is now no condemnation for those who are in Christ Jesus." (Romans 8:1, NIV)

In Christ, our old identity as sinners has been completely replaced by a new identity as saints—set apart by God, forgiven, and loved. This shift from sinner to saint is not about denying our past but embracing the radical transformation that Christ has brought. We no longer have to live under the weight of guilt or shame, but instead can walk in the freedom of our new identity. Understanding that there is no condemnation frees us to live confidently and fully in the grace Christ has given us.

The Last Ash: You are no longer defined by your mistakes in Christ. How does it affect the way you live?

The Final Sip: How does this freedom enable you to live with purpose, knowing that your past is forgiven, and you are free to walk in God's grace?

July 9

Becoming a Man After God's Own Heart

"After removing Saul, he made David their king. God testified concerning him: 'I have found David son of Jesse, a man after my own heart; he will do everything I want him to do.'"
(Acts 13:22, NIV)

David was not perfect, but his heart was aligned with God's will. To be a man after God's own heart is to seek God's desires above all else, to be passionate about His will, and to be obedient, even when it is difficult. This pursuit involves humility, repentance, and a commitment to grow in relationship with God.

The Last Ash: Being a man after God's own heart is about aligning your heart with His. How can you live out this pursuit through obedience, humility, and a sincere desire to know Him more deeply?

**The Final Sip:** How can you intentionally seek to align your heart with God's desires today to grow closer to Him?

July 10

Living in True Freedom

"It is for freedom that Christ has set us free. Stand firm, then, and do not let yourselves be burdened again by a yoke of slavery." (Galatians 5:1, NIV)

He set us free from the bondage of sin and the burden of trying to earn God's approval through rules and rituals. This verse calls us to stand firm in that freedom and resist anything that tries to drag us back into spiritual slavery. It is a reminder that true freedom isn't about doing whatever we want—it's about living in the power and grace Christ provides, free from fear, guilt, and legalism.

**The Last Ash:** In what areas of your life do you still struggle to fully embrace the freedom Christ offers?

The Final Sip: How can this truth help you step forward with confidence and clarity today, knowing that your identity is rooted in Christ?

July 11

Living as an Ambassador for Christ

"We are therefore Christ's ambassadors, as though God were making his appeal through us. We implore you on Christ's behalf: Be reconciled to God." (2 Corinthians 5:20, NIV)

As believers, we are called to represent Christ in every area of our lives. An ambassador carries the authority of the one they represent, and similarly, we carry the authority of Christ, speaking on His behalf and urging others to be reconciled to God. Our actions, words, and attitudes reflect Christ to those around us.

The Last Ash: Do you live in a way that reflects Christ's love and message? How can you represent Him more faithfully?

The Final Sip: In what ways can you faithfully live out your role as Christ's representative, ensuring that your actions and words draw others toward Him?

July 12

The Strength of Being Set Apart

"Do not conform to the pattern of this world, but be transformed by the renewing of your mind. Then you will be able to test and approve what God's will is—his good, pleasing, and perfect will." (Romans 12:2, NIV)

Being set apart for God's purposes requires a conscious decision to resist the pressures of the world around us. When we stop conforming to worldly patterns and allow God's Word to shape our thinking, we gain strength and clarity to follow His will. Being set apart is not about isolation but about living with purpose, focused on God's desires rather than the world's distractions.

The Last Ash: How can you consciously resist the pull of worldly conformity?

The Final Sip: How has God renewed your mind and actions, and how can you continue to grow in this transformation as you live out His purpose for you?

July 13

Trusting God with Your Failures

"My flesh and my heart may fail, but God is the strength of my heart and my portion forever." (Psalm 73:26, NIV)

During failure, God's strength is unshaken. Trusting God during our failures allows us to experience His restoration and grace. He is the one who strengthens us when we are weak, and He is our portion, providing us with all we need, even in our brokenness. God's faithfulness remains constant, and in Him, we find hope and strength to rise again.

The Last Ash: How did trusting God during that time help you grow stronger and more reliant on Him?

The Final Sip: How can you surrender your failures to God and allow Him to strengthen you for the journey ahead?

July 14

More Than Conquerors in Christ

"No, in all these things we are more than conquerors through him who loved us." (Romans 8:37, NIV)

As believers, we are more than conquerors—not because of our own strength but through Christ who loves us. The battles may be difficult, but Christ has already won the ultimate victory. His love empowers us to overcome challenges and live in the freedom He offers, walking in triumph over sin and circumstances.

The Last Ash: How does this truth reshape your perspective on difficulties and setbacks? In what areas of your life can you walk in the victory Christ has already won for you?

The Final Sip: How can you claim the victory over sin and adversity, trusting that Christ's love and strength will carry you through?

July 15

God's Unchanging Love for You

"I have loved you with an everlasting love; I have drawn you with unfailing kindness." (Jeremiah 31:3, NIV)

God's love is not fleeting or conditional; it is everlasting and unfailing. His love is not based on our actions or worthiness but on His nature, which is unchanging. This truth provides us with security and peace because we know that God's love is always present, no matter what we face. His kindness continuously draws us closer to Him, and in His love, we find true rest and assurance.

The Last Ash: How does knowing God loves you with an everlasting love change the way you approach life's uncertainties and challenges?

The Final Sip: How can you rest in His love today, knowing that it is constant and never fails, no matter the circumstances?

July 16

Strength in Surrender – Letting Go and Trusting God

"Trust in the Lord with all your heart and lean not on your own understanding; in all your ways submit to him, and he will make your paths straight." (Proverbs 3:5-6, NIV)

Surrendering control to God requires trusting Him completely, even when we don't understand the path ahead. When we trust Him, He promises to direct our paths. Surrender doesn't mean passivity—it's an active choice to let God lead. In surrender, we find peace and direction that surpasses our own limited perspective, knowing that God's plan is always best.

 **The Last Ash:** How can trusting God bring peace?

 **The Final Sip:** How can you trust God's direction today, even in situations that feel unclear or out of your control?

July 17

Walking in Trust Even When You Can't See the Way

"For we live by faith, not by sight." (2 Corinthians 5:7, NIV)

Living by faith is about trusting in God's unseen promises and stepping forward without needing all the answers. It challenges us to rely on God's guidance even when we can't see the full picture. This type of faith pushes us beyond the limits of our natural understanding, requiring us to trust God in the unknown and uncertain moments of life. By walking in trust, we deepen our dependence on Him, and our relationship with God grows stronger.

The Last Ash: Reflect on a time when you had to trust God despite not seeing the way. How did that experience impact your trust in Him?

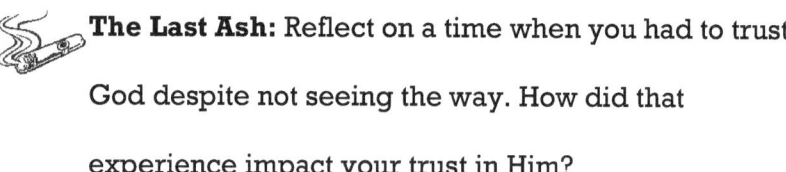

The Final Sip: How can you embrace faith over sight today and allow your relationship with God to deepen through trust?

July 18

Guarding Against Division

"For I am afraid that when I come I may not find you as I want you to be, and you may not find me as you want me to be. I fear that there may be discord, jealousy, fits of rage, selfish ambition, slander, gossip, arrogance, and disorder."
(2 Corinthians 12:20, NIV)

This is a sobering reminder of the dangers that can creep into our lives and relationships—discord, jealousy, anger, and selfish ambition. Paul's concern is not just for individual actions but for how these behaviors can destroy unity and trust within a community. For men striving to lead with integrity, this verse challenges us to examine our hearts and relationships, addressing any attitudes that might cause division or harm.

The Last Ash: What attitudes or actions in your life could be causing tension or division with others?

The Final Sip: How can you promote peace and unity in your relationships?

July 19

The Power of Speaking Life

"Gracious words are a honeycomb, sweet to the soul and healing to the bones." (Proverbs 16:24, NIV)

Words have the power to bring life or death to a situation, and Proverbs 16:24 emphasizes the sweetness and healing that come from gracious words. When we speak life, encouragement, and truth, we not only bless those around us but also shape our own hearts and minds. Words are powerful tools that can build others up and bring healing, fostering deeper relationships and spreading positivity.

The Last Ash: How can you use your words today to bring healing and encouragement to those around you?

The Final Sip: How can you practice speaking life today, and how might this influence your interactions with others?

July 20

Trusting God for Joy and Protection

"The Lord is my strength and my shield; my heart trusts in him, and he helps me. My heart leaps for joy, and with my song I praise him." (Psalm 28:7, NIV)

When we place our trust in Him, He doesn't just leave us to fight alone—He steps in and helps us. This verse shows a progression: trust leads to God's help, which results in joy and praise. David's heart overflows with gratitude because he recognizes God's faithful intervention. For men seeking to lead with courage and integrity, this verse is a powerful reminder that true strength comes from trusting God. When we rely on Him, joy follows, and our natural response should be to praise Him.

The Last Ash: In what areas of your life do you need to trust God more as your strength and shield?

The Final Sip: How can you turn your gratitude for God's help into praise and encouragement for others?

July 21

The Pursuit of Peace

"If it is possible, as far as it depends on you, live at peace with everyone." (Romans 12:18, NIV)

This is a call to take responsibility for our actions and attitudes, striving to be agents of reconciliation rather than division. For men leading in their families, workplaces, and communities, this requires humility, patience, and a willingness to let go of pride or the need to always be right. Living at peace is a sign of strength and maturity, reflecting the heart of Christ in a world often filled with conflict.

The Last Ash: What steps can you take to promote peace in a difficult relationship or situation?

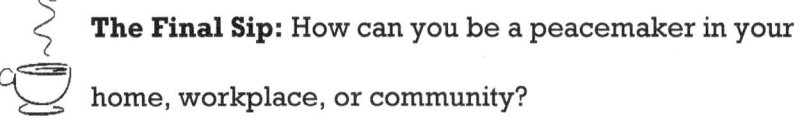

The Final Sip: How can you be a peacemaker in your home, workplace, or community?

July 22

God's Peace in the Storm

"Peace I leave with you; my peace I give you. I do not give to you as the world gives. Do not let your hearts be troubled and do not be afraid." (John 14:27, NIV)

God's peace is unlike anything the world offers. It is deep and unshakable, given to us by Jesus, even in the midst of life's storms. In this verse, Jesus assures His followers that His peace will calm our hearts, providing comfort and courage despite external circumstances. Trusting in His peace allows us to rest in His presence, even when everything around us feels unstable.

 **The Last Ash:** How can you intentionally remind yourself of God's peace when facing difficult situations?

The Final Sip: What steps can you take today to experience peace, even in the midst of challenges?

July 23

Love in Action – Demonstrating Christ's Love Daily

"Dear children, let us not love with words or speech but with actions and in truth." (1 John 3:18, NIV)

True love is not just spoken—it is demonstrated through our actions. John emphasizes that love must be active and sincere, reflecting God's love for us. By serving others, showing kindness, and speaking truth in love, we make God's love tangible to those around us. Christ's love calls us to go beyond just saying "I love you" and move into genuine acts of care and sacrifice for others.

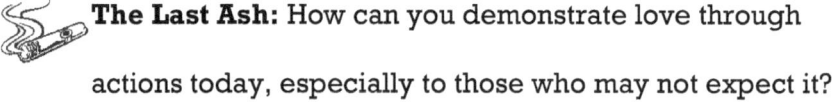 **The Last Ash:** How can you demonstrate love through actions today, especially to those who may not expect it?

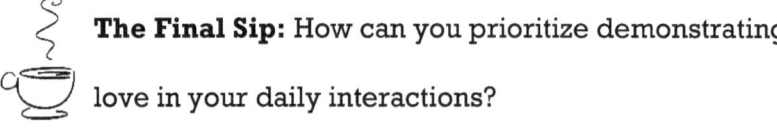 **The Final Sip:** How can you prioritize demonstrating love in your daily interactions?

July 24

Finding Joy in the Journey – Rejoicing in Every Season of Life

"Consider it pure joy, my brothers and sisters, whenever you face trials of many kinds, because you know that the testing of your faith produces perseverance." (James 1:2-3, NIV)

James challenges us to find joy in trials, knowing that they strengthen our faith and build perseverance. Trials are not easy, but they are opportunities to grow in character and trust in God. When we choose joy, even in difficult times, we align ourselves with God's greater purpose for our lives. The joy doesn't come from the trial itself but from the growth and maturity that results from enduring it with faith.

 **The Last Ash:** How can you view current challenges as opportunities for growth and perseverance?

The Final Sip: How can you cultivate an attitude of joy today, even in difficult circumstances?

July 25

Breaking Free from Fear – Choosing Faith Over Anxiety

"For the Spirit God gave us does not make us timid, but gives us power, love and self-discipline." (2 Timothy 1:7, NIV)

Fear is not from God; He has given us a spirit of power, love, and self-discipline to overcome it. When we face fear, God empowers us to stand firm, trusting in His strength. Anxiety and timidity give way to courage, grounded in the love and discipline that the Holy Spirit offers. By choosing faith over fear, we step into the boldness that comes from knowing we are secure in God's care.

 **The Last Ash:** In what areas of your life do you need to choose faith over fear today?

The Final Sip: How can you embrace God's power today to overcome fear and move forward with confidence?

July 26

Following God's Commands Brings Fulfillment

"If you fully obey the Lord your God and carefully follow all his commands I give you today, the Lord your God will set you high above all the nations on earth. All these blessings will come upon you and accompany you if you obey the Lord your God." (Deuteronomy 28:1-2, NIV)

Obedience to God's commands is not just about following rules—it is about positioning ourselves to receive His blessings. When we obey God, we open the door for His favor and guidance. The blessings mentioned in these verses go beyond material gain; they include peace, wisdom, and a deeper relationship with Him. True fulfillment comes when we align our lives with God's will.

The Last Ash: How can you align your actions more closely with God's commands today?

The Final Sip: How can you embrace obedience to God in a way that brings fulfillment and blesses others around you?

July 27

Loving Like Jesus Through Acts of Service

"Jesus looked at him and loved him. 'One thing you lack,' he said. 'Go, sell everything you have and give to the poor, and you will have treasure in heaven. Then come, follow me.'"
(Mark 10:21, NIV)

Though he lived a moral life, Jesus saw that his possessions had a hold on his heart. This verse is a reminder that following Christ requires surrendering anything that competes for our devotion. For men, this call can feel difficult—we often place security in success, wealth, or control. But Jesus offers something far greater: eternal treasure and a life of purpose. True freedom comes when we let go of what holds us back and fully follow Him.

The Last Ash: What's one thing in your life that may be holding you back from fully following Christ?

The Final Sip: How can you practice generosity and trust God more with your resources?

July 28

Waiting on God's Timing – Trusting That His Plan is Perfect

"But those who hope in the Lord will renew their strength. They will soar on wings like eagles; they will run and not grow weary, they will walk and not be faint." (Isaiah 40:31, NIV)

Waiting on God's timing requires patience and trust. When we hope in the Lord, He renews our strength, allowing us to endure and rise above life's challenges. God's plan is always perfect and waiting on His timing leads to deeper strength and spiritual growth. In our impatience, we may try to rush things, but God's perfect timing results in the best outcome for us.

 **The Last Ash:** How can you surrender your impatience and trust in God's perfect plan today?

The Final Sip: What areas of your life require patience, and how can you rest in God's perfect timing?

July 29

Shifting Your Perspective Through Thankfulness

"Enter his gates with thanksgiving and his courts with praise; give thanks to him and praise his name." (Psalm 100:4, NIV)

Gratitude shifts our perspective, drawing us closer to God. Thankfulness is a powerful tool for worship, helping us focus on God's goodness and provision. When we enter His presence with thanksgiving, our hearts align with His will, and we are reminded of His faithfulness. Gratitude helps us embrace life with joy, even in challenging circumstances, and opens the door to deeper worship.

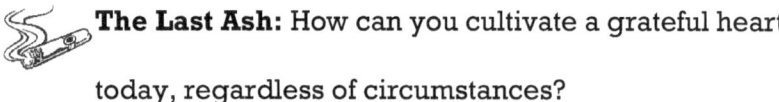**The Last Ash:** How can you cultivate a grateful heart today, regardless of circumstances?

**The Final Sip:** What are you grateful for today, and how can you express that thankfulness to God?

July 30

Letting Go of Pride to Serve God Fully

"He has shown you, O mortal, what is good. And what does the Lord require of you? To act justly and to love mercy and to walk humbly with your God." (Micah 6:8, NIV)

Humility is central to our relationship with God and others. When we let go of pride, we create space for God's work to be done in and through us. Humility isn't about thinking less of ourselves but thinking of ourselves less—putting others and God's will before our own desires. By walking in humility, we open ourselves up to serving God fully and reflecting His character to the world.

The Last Ash: How can you practice humility in your relationships with others and with God today?

The Final Sip:

How might your relationships and leadership be transformed by a deeper humility?

July 31

Prioritizing God in Every Aspect of Life

"But seek first his kingdom and his righteousness, and all these things will be given to you as well." (Matthew 6:33, NIV)

Jesus calls us to seek God's kingdom and righteousness first, promising that everything else will fall into place. When we focus on aligning our lives with His desires, everything else—our needs, our worries, our plans—becomes secondary. Seeking God first brings clarity and peace because it shifts our focus away from the distractions of life to the eternal purpose He has for us. In doing so, we trust that God will provide for us in ways beyond what we could imagine.

The Last Ash: In what areas of your life can you shift your focus to seek God more fully?

The Final Sip: How can you actively choose to prioritize God in every aspect of your life today?

August

The Power of Prayer

This month, we focus on being bold and believing in prayer.

August 1

Praying with Boldness

"Let us then approach God's throne of grace with confidence, so that we may receive mercy and find grace to help us in our time of need." (Hebrews 4:16, NIV)

Boldness in prayer doesn't mean demanding or treating God as a servant but rather approaching with confidence in His love and willingness to help. It changes how we approach life's challenges and opportunities because it reminds us that we have access to the Creator of the universe, who is both powerful and merciful.

The Last Ash: How does boldly approaching God's throne in prayer transform challenges into opportunities for His strength and mercy?

The Final Sip: How can we build confidence in prayer by trusting God's promises?

August 2

When God Seems Silent

"Wait for the Lord; be strong and take heart and wait for the Lord." (Psalm 27:14, NIV)

In moments of silence, waiting for the Lord requires both patience and trust. It is during these times that God often works in the background, building our faith, patience, and reliance on Him. When answers are delayed, it can be a test of our perseverance and trust in God's perfect timing.

The Last Ash: Waiting on the Lord in silence strengthens our faith by teaching us to trust in His timing and purpose, even when we can't see the immediate results.

The Final Sip: Trusting God's silence allows us to grow in our relationship with Him, knowing that His plans are always for our good, even when we don't understand His delay.

August 3

Praying for Your Family

"When a period of feasting had run its course, Job would make arrangements for them to be purified. Early in the morning he would sacrifice a burnt offering for each of them, thinking, 'Perhaps my children have sinned and cursed God in their hearts.' This was Job's regular custom." (Job 1:5, NIV)

Job's dedication to praying for his children's spiritual well-being is an example of how parents should intercede for their families. His concern was not just for their physical needs, but for their relationship with God. This highlights the importance of covering our families in prayer, seeking God's protection and guidance for them.

The Last Ash: How can Job's example inspire us to pray persistently for our loved ones?

The Final Sip: How do daily prayers for your family invite God's protection and grace?

August 4

The Lord's Prayer: A Model for Communication

"This, then, is how you should pray: 'Our Father in heaven, hallowed be your name, your kingdom come, your will be done, on earth as it is in heaven. Give us today our daily bread. And forgive us our debts, as we also have forgiven our debtors. And lead us not into temptation, but deliver us from the evil one.'" (Matthew 6:9-13, NIV)

The Lord's Prayer offers a powerful framework for how we should communicate with God. It teaches us to honor God's holiness, seek His will, ask for daily provisions, confess our sins, and request His protection. It serves as a guide that covers all aspects of life and spirituality, helping to center our prayers on God's purposes.

 The Last Ash: How does the Lord's Prayer balance reverence and intimacy with God?

 **The Final Sip:** How does the Lord's Prayer help us stay focused and mindful in prayer?

August 5

Trusting God's Answers to Your Prayers

"This is the confidence we have in approaching God: that if we ask anything according to his will, he hears us. And if we know that he hears us—whatever we ask—we know that we have what we asked of him." (1 John 5:14-15, NIV)

This passage teaches us to trust that God hears our prayers and will answer according to His will, which is always good. Trusting His answers requires surrendering our expectations and recognizing that He knows what is best for us, even when the outcome is different from what we imagined.

The Last Ash: How does trusting God's answers strengthen our faith?

The Final Sip: How does knowing God answers according to His will bring peace?

August 6

The Power of Praying Scripture

"So is my word that goes out from my mouth: It will not return to me empty, but will accomplish what I desire and achieve the purpose for which I sent it." (Isaiah 55:11, NIV)

Praying Scripture aligns our hearts with God's will because His Word is powerful and effective. When we pray God's promises, we are engaging in a divine conversation that allows His Word to shape our circumstances. This is a reminder that His Word is never void of power—it always accomplishes His purposes.

The Last Ash: How does praying Scripture align our requests with God's promises?

The Final Sip: How does praying Scripture empower and transform us?

August 7

Responding with Grace

"Bless those who curse you, pray for those who mistreat you."
(Luke 6:28, NIV)

Blessing those who curse us and praying for those who mistreat us is not a sign of weakness but of incredible strength and maturity. This command reflects the heart of Christ, who taught us to love our enemies and trust God to work in every situation. As men striving to live with purpose and integrity, this verse reminds us that true leadership often means choosing mercy over revenge and prayer over resentment.

The Last Ash: How can you bless someone who has wronged you?

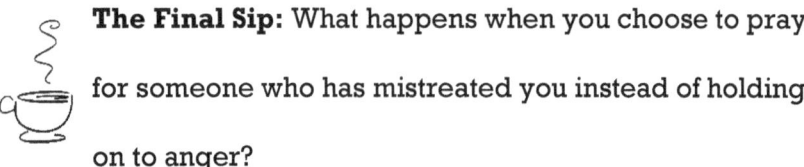

The Final Sip: What happens when you choose to pray for someone who has mistreated you instead of holding on to anger?

August 8

Interceding for Others

"I urge, then, first of all, that petitions, prayers, intercession, and thanksgiving be made for all people" (1 Timothy 2:1, NIV)

Intercession is the act of praying on behalf of others. In this verse, Paul urges us to prioritize praying for people, lifting their needs and concerns to God. Interceding for others deepens our connection with God because it requires selflessness and empathy, aligning our hearts with His. When we pray for others, we also strengthen our faith in God's ability to bring change and answer prayers. Intercession is an expression of love and care for others, reflecting Christ's heart for those in need.

 The Last Ash: How does interceding for others deepen your connection with God and strengthen your faith in His power to change lives?

 **The Final Sip:** How can making others' needs a priority in prayer reflect Christ's love for those around you?

August 9

Persistent Prayer Pays Off

"Then Jesus told his disciples a parable to show them that they should always pray and not give up." (Luke 18:1, NIV)

Persistence in prayer is an essential part of our relationship with God. This parable encourages us to continue praying, even when we don't see immediate results. Jesus highlights that persistent prayer not only demonstrates our trust in God but also strengthens our perseverance. By continually seeking God, we are reminded that He is faithful and that His timing is perfect. The more we pray, the more our faith grows, and our relationship with God deepens.

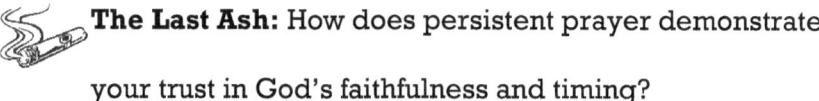

The Last Ash: How does persistent prayer demonstrate your trust in God's faithfulness and timing?

The Final Sip: How can consistent prayer build your patience and perseverance, knowing that God honors your faithfulness?

August 10

Gratitude in Prayer

"Devote yourselves to prayer, being watchful and thankful."
(Colossians 4:2, NIV)

Gratitude is a powerful element in prayer. Paul urges us to be devoted to prayer, making sure that our prayers are infused with thankfulness. When we express gratitude in our prayers, we are reminded of all that God has done for us. Gratitude shifts our focus from what we lack to the abundance of blessings in our lives, helping us maintain a heart of contentment. This practice also deepens our relationship with God as we recognize His constant goodness and provision.

The Last Ash: How can incorporating gratitude into your prayers deepen your awareness of God's goodness in every situation?

The Final Sip: How does expressing thanks to God in prayer cultivate a heart of contentment and joy?

August 11

Praying for Wisdom in Hard Decisions

"If any of you lacks wisdom, let him ask of God, who gives to all liberally and without reproach, and it will be given to him." (James 1:5, NIV)

Making tough decisions can often leave us feeling uncertain and lost. However, James assures us that if we lack wisdom, we can ask God, who gives generously to those who seek it. Prayer is a way to humbly acknowledge our need for God's guidance and wisdom. When we pray for wisdom, we are reminded that God is always ready to help us make decisions that align with His will. In times of uncertainty, seeking His wisdom through prayer provides clarity and confidence.

The Last Ash: How can seeking God's wisdom in prayer guide you through tough choices and uncertainty?

The Final Sip: How does trusting God for wisdom in decision-making help you navigate life with confidence and clarity?

August 12

Prayers of Confession and Restoration

"Create in me a pure heart, O God, and renew a steadfast spirit within me." (Psalm 51:10, NIV)

Confession is an essential part of our relationship with God, as it allows us to acknowledge our sin and seek His forgiveness. In this psalm, David pleads for God to create in him a pure heart and renew his spirit. Prayer of confession brings healing, restoration, and renewal, allowing us to experience the freedom that comes from being forgiven. When we confess our sins, God is faithful to cleanse us, drawing us closer to Him and helping us grow in our walk with Him.

The Last Ash: How does confessing your sins in prayer lead to God's forgiveness and restoration?

The Final Sip: How can honest prayers of confession bring healing and renewal in your relationship with God?

August 13

Prayer That Changes Your Perspective

"Our God, will you not judge them? For we have no power to face this vast army that is attacking us. We do not know what to do, but our eyes are upon you." (2 Chronicles 20:12, NIV)

When facing overwhelming situations, it's easy to feel helpless and lost. By turning to God, he shifts his focus from the problem to the solution: God's sovereignty. Prayer helps us align our hearts with God's will, moving our gaze from the problem to His power and provision. It shifts our fear to faith, knowing that God is in control even when the situation seems impossible.

The Last Ash: How can prayer change your perspective when facing overwhelming situations or obstacles?

The Final Sip: How does turning to prayer during times of uncertainty shift your focus from fear to faith in God's sovereignty?

August 14

Listening for God's Voice in Prayer

"My sheep listen to my voice; I know them, and they follow me." (John 10:27, NIV)

Prayer is not only about speaking to God, but also about listening to His voice. Jesus compares His followers to sheep who know and listen to their Shepherd's voice. In prayer, we cultivate a listening heart, attuned to God's guidance and direction. Listening is an active process, requiring quietness and attentiveness to hear God's whispers. When we listen to God, we open ourselves to His guidance, helping us follow His lead in every aspect of our lives.

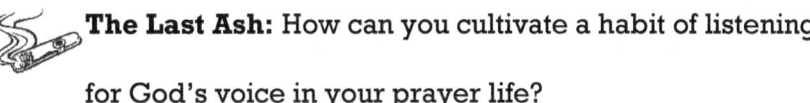**The Last Ash:** How can you cultivate a habit of listening for God's voice in your prayer life?

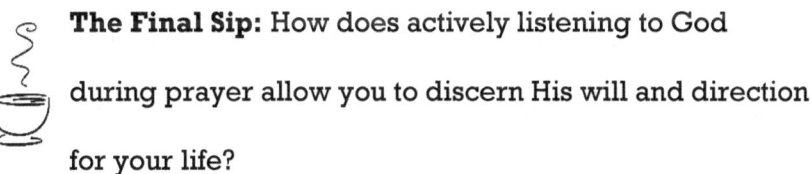**The Final Sip:** How does actively listening to God during prayer allow you to discern His will and direction for your life?

August 15

Finding Peace in the Quiet Place

"But when you pray, go into your room, close the door and pray to your Father, who is unseen; then your Father, who sees what is done in secret, will reward you." (Matthew 6:6, NIV)

Jesus teaches us the importance of solitude and quietness in prayer. By retreating to a quiet place, free from distractions, we create space to focus solely on God. In these moments, we can experience peace that surpasses understanding. Prayer in the quiet place allows us to tune out the noise of the world and center our hearts on God. In the stillness, we can hear God more clearly, and His peace fills us, restoring our souls.

The Last Ash: How can creating quiet moments in your prayer time help you find peace amidst life's chaos?

The Final Sip: How does retreating to a quiet space to pray strengthen your inner peace and deepen your connection with God?

August 16

Building a Strong Foundation of Faith

"He replied, 'Because you have so little faith. Truly I tell you, if you have faith as small as a mustard seed, you can say to this mountain, "Move from here to there," and it will move. Nothing will be impossible for you.'" (Matthew 17:20, NIV)

This scripture reveals how even the smallest amount of faith can lead to extraordinary results when paired with prayer. Jesus emphasizes that faith in God's power, no matter how small, can overcome any obstacle. Prayer nurtures this faith by focusing our hearts and minds on God's strength, helping us see beyond our limitations and trust in His ability to accomplish what we cannot.

The Last Ash: How can prayer strengthen your faith and help you overcome doubts and uncertainties?

The Final Sip: How does cultivating a prayerful life help you build an unshakable faith in God's power and promises?

August 17

Living a Spirit-Filled Prayer Life

"In the same way, the Spirit helps us in our weakness. We do not know what we ought to pray for, but the Spirit himself intercedes for us through wordless groans." (Romans 8:26, NIV)

When we pray, the Holy Spirit comes alongside us, guiding our prayers even when we feel inadequate or overwhelmed. This scripture highlights the importance of surrendering to the Holy Spirit in prayer, allowing Him to intercede on our behalf. A spirit-filled prayer life connects us deeply with God's will and strengthens our relationship with Him, especially in times of weakness.

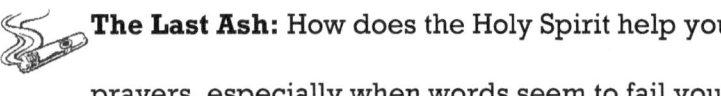 **The Last Ash:** How does the Holy Spirit help you in your prayers, especially when words seem to fail you?

 **The Final Sip:** How can surrendering to the Holy Spirit's guidance in prayer deepen your relationship with God?

August 18

Seeking God's Safeguard

"He will cover you with his feathers, and under his wings you will find refuge; his faithfulness will be your shield and rampart." (Psalm 91:4, NIV)

God's protection is a constant theme throughout the Bible. In this verse, He promises to shield us with His faithfulness and provide refuge during times of fear or danger. Praying for protection invites God's presence into our situations, granting us peace and courage.

The Last Ash: How does praying for God's protection bring peace when facing uncertainty or danger?

The Final Sip: How can trusting God's promises for safety strengthen your courage in times of fear?

August 19

Believing in God's Healing Power

"And the prayer offered in faith will make the sick person well; the Lord will raise them up. If they have sinned, they will be forgiven." (James 5:15, NIV)

This verse affirms the healing power of prayer, reminding us that God's ability to restore physical health is inseparable from His ability to heal spiritually. Faith-filled prayers not only bring restoration to our bodies but also to our souls, as we seek His forgiveness.

The Last Ash: How does prayer for healing demonstrate your trust in God's ability to restore both body and soul?

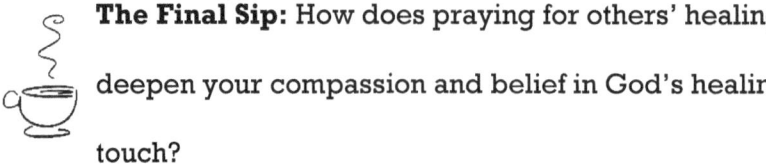

The Final Sip: How does praying for others' healing deepen your compassion and belief in God's healing touch?

August 20

Releasing the Burden of Unforgiveness

"And when you stand praying, if you hold anything against anyone, forgive them, so that your Father in heaven may forgive you your sins." (Mark 11:25, NIV)

Forgiveness is a central theme in the Christian faith, and this verse highlights how it relates to our prayer life. Unforgiveness creates a barrier between us and God. When we forgive others in prayer, we align our hearts with God's mercy, allowing His forgiveness to flow into our lives.

The Last Ash: How can prayer help you release bitterness and forgive those who have wronged you?

The Final Sip: How does forgiving others in prayer align your heart with God's grace and mercy?

August 21

Fighting Spiritual Battles Through Prayer

"And pray in the Spirit on all occasions with all kinds of prayers and requests. With this in mind, be alert and always keep on praying for all the Lord's people." (Ephesians 6:18, NIV)

This scripture emphasizes the importance of prayer as a weapon in spiritual warfare. Prayer is our defense against the enemy's attacks, and it is through consistent and vigilant prayer that we can stand firm in our faith. Spiritual battles are fought and won in prayer, as we rely on God's strength to overcome the darkness.

 **The Last Ash:** How does prayer become a weapon against the spiritual forces that oppose you?

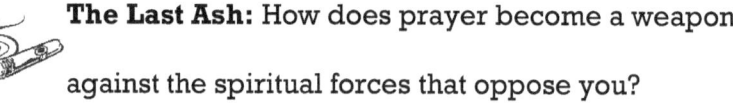 **The Final Sip:** How can standing firm in prayer help you find victory over temptation and spiritual attack?

August 22

The Power of Agreement in Prayer

"Again, truly I tell you that if two of you on earth agree about anything they ask for, it will be done for them by my Father in heaven." (Matthew 18:19, NIV)

This verse highlights the power of unity in prayer. When two or more believers come together in agreement, their prayers are amplified. Prayer partnerships create an atmosphere of faith and expectation, leading to greater impact as God moves in response to collective faith.

**The Last Ash:** How does praying in agreement with others amplify the power of prayer?

The Final Sip: How can finding a prayer partner enhance your faith and lead to breakthroughs in your life?

August 23

Let Peace Lead

"Let the peace of Christ rule in your hearts, since as members of one body you were called to peace. And be thankful."
(Colossians 3:15, NIV)

Peace isn't about the absence of problems but the presence of Christ in every situation. As men, we often face pressure to control outcomes, but this verse reminds us that true peace comes from trusting God, not our circumstances. When Christ's peace rules in our hearts, we respond with patience and grace, fostering unity and gratitude in our relationships and communities.

 **The Last Ash:** What areas of your life need to be ruled by Christ's peace instead of fear or control?

The Final Sip: How can practicing gratitude help you experience more of God's peace?

August 24

Asking God for What You Need

"Do not be anxious about anything, but in every situation, by prayer and petition, with thanksgiving, present your requests to God." (Philippians 4:6, NIV)

This scripture invites us to bring all our needs before God through prayer and petition. Rather than allowing anxiety to overwhelm us, we are encouraged to present our requests with a heart of thanksgiving, recognizing God's faithfulness. Asking God for what we need strengthens our trust in His provision, aligning our hearts with His will.

The Last Ash: How does praying with boldness and clarity in your requests strengthen your trust in God's provision?

The Final Sip: How can laying your petitions before God bring clarity and peace, knowing He hears your every need?

August 25

Praying for the Body of Christ

"For this reason, since the day we heard about you, we have not stopped praying for you. We continually ask God to fill you with the knowledge of his will through all the wisdom and understanding that the Spirit gives." (Colossians 1:9, NIV)

In this verse, Paul prays earnestly for the Colossians, asking God to fill them with wisdom and understanding. Similarly, praying for your church family is an act of love and intercession that unites the body of Christ. When we pray for one another, we strengthen the unity of the church and align ourselves with God's mission for His people.

The Last Ash: How does praying for your church family unite you in purpose and strengthen your support of one another?

The Final Sip: How can consistent prayers for your church foster spiritual growth and strengthen its mission?

August 26

United by Grace

"It is right for me to feel this way about all of you, since I have you in my heart and, whether I am in chains or defending and confirming the gospel, all of you share in God's grace with me." (Philippians 1:7, NIV)

Philippians 1:7 reveals Paul's deep love and connection with the believers in Philippi. Despite his difficult circumstances—whether in chains or defending the gospel—Paul reminds them that they are partners in God's grace. This verse highlights the unbreakable bond we have with others through our shared faith. For men, it's a call to recognize and cherish the relationships God places in our lives.

The Last Ash: Who in your life has been a partner in God's grace, encouraging and supporting you in your journey?

The Final Sip: How can you strengthen your connection with other men of faith and support them in their walk with God?

August 27

Turning Back to God

"If we confess our sins, he is faithful and just and will forgive us our sins and purify us from all unrighteousness."
(1 John 1:9, NIV)

Repentance restores our relationship with God and renews our hearts. This verse reminds us that when we confess our sins in prayer, God is faithful to forgive and purify us. Prayer of repentance is a transformative act that leads to spiritual renewal and a closer walk with God.

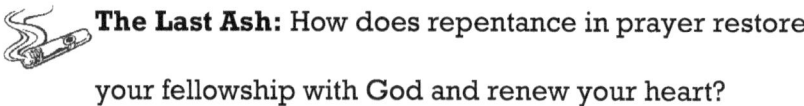

The Last Ash: How does repentance in prayer restore your fellowship with God and renew your heart?

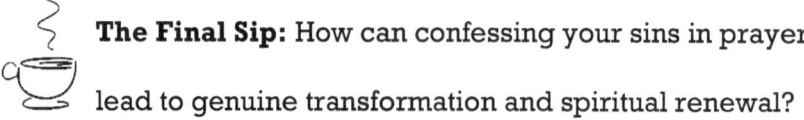

The Final Sip: How can confessing your sins in prayer lead to genuine transformation and spiritual renewal?

August 28

Praying with a Heart of Joy

"You make known to me the path of life; you will fill me with joy in your presence, with eternal pleasures at your right hand." (Psalm 16:11, NIV)

This verse speaks of the joy found in God's presence. Prayer is an opportunity to connect with God's joy, filling our hearts with His peace and delight. When we pray with joy, our relationship with God deepens, and we reflect His joy to those around us, inspiring others to seek His presence as well.

The Last Ash: How can joy in prayer transform your relationship with God and inspire others around you?

The Final Sip: How does embracing joy in prayer open your heart to experience the fullness of God's presence?

August 29

Praying for Souls to be Saved

"The Lord is not slow in keeping his promise, as some understand slowness. Instead, he is patient with you, not wanting anyone to perish, but everyone to come to repentance." (2 Peter 3:9, NIV)

God's desire for all to be saved motivates us to pray for the lost. When we intercede for others, we align our hearts with His mission of salvation. Prayer for the lost demonstrates compassion and reflects God's patient love, reminding us that He is giving time for repentance and salvation.

The Last Ash: How can praying for the lost reflect your heart for God's mission in the world?

The Final Sip: How does making the salvation of others a priority in prayer deepen your compassion for those who don't know Christ?

August 30

Seeking Renewal in Your Life and Community

"If my people, who are called by my name, will humble themselves and pray and seek my face and turn from their wicked ways, then I will hear from heaven, and I will forgive their sin and will heal their land." (2 Chronicles 7:14, NIV)

This verse is a call for repentance and prayer for national and spiritual renewal. Revival begins with prayer—humbling ourselves, seeking God's face, and turning from sin. When we pray for revival, we seek God's transformation in our lives and in our communities, inviting His healing and renewal.

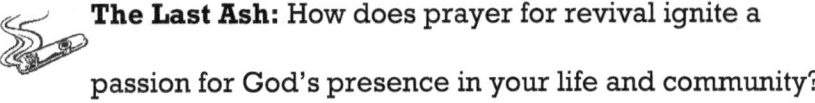

The Last Ash: How does prayer for revival ignite a passion for God's presence in your life and community?

The Final Sip: How can praying for spiritual awakening in your heart and the world lead to transformation?

August 31

Staying Consistent in Prayer Daily

"Pray continually." (1 Thessalonians 5:17, NIV)

This simple yet profound verse encourages us to make prayer a constant part of our lives. Consistent prayer nurtures our relationship with God, strengthens our faith, and aligns our hearts with His will. Living a life of prayer means staying connected to God throughout each day, trusting in His provision and guidance.

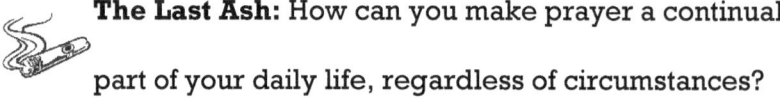

The Last Ash: How can you make prayer a continual part of your daily life, regardless of circumstances?

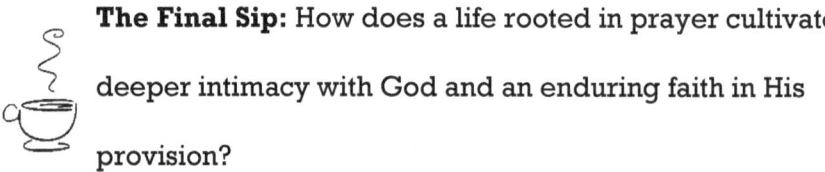

The Final Sip: How does a life rooted in prayer cultivate deeper intimacy with God and an enduring faith in His provision?

September

Overcoming Spiritual Battles

The fight is real.

This month we will fight the good fight and win.

September 1

Recognizing the Enemy's Schemes

"In order that Satan might not outwit us. For we are not unaware of his schemes." (2 Corinthians 2:11, NIV)

The enemy is constantly strategizing to lead us astray, often through subtle tactics that we may not even recognize in the moment. But the good news is, God has equipped us with wisdom and discernment through His Word, making us aware of the enemy's ways. Understanding his schemes enables us to be proactive in resisting his influence, remaining rooted in God's truth.

The Last Ash: How can being aware of the enemy's tactics help you stand firm in your faith and resist his attacks?

The Final Sip: How does recognizing the enemy's schemes allow you to protect your heart and mind from his influence?

September 2

Fighting Temptation with Truth

"Jesus answered, 'It is written: Man shall not live on bread alone, but on every word that comes from the mouth of God.'" (Matthew 4:4, NIV)

In times of temptation, Jesus exemplified the power of speaking the truth of God's Word to counter the lies of the enemy. His response to Satan's temptations reminds us that God's Word is not just knowledge, but a weapon we can use to stand firm in our faith. In moments of temptation, we must remember that God's truth is our sustenance, stronger than any earthly need.

The Last Ash: How can speaking God's truth combat the temptation to stray from His will?

The Final Sip: How can you use Scripture to stand strong in the face of temptation and trust God's provision?

September 3

The Sword of the Spirit: Your Greatest Weapon

"Take the helmet of salvation and the sword of the Spirit, which is the word of God." (Ephesians 6:17, NIV)

The Bible is not just a book of stories or wisdom; it is the Sword of the Spirit, our greatest weapon in spiritual warfare. It has the power to cut through the lies and deceptions of the enemy, protecting our hearts and minds from his attacks. When we immerse ourselves in the Scriptures, we strengthen our ability to resist the enemy and stand victorious in the battles we face.

The Last Ash: How does God's Word, as the Sword of the Spirit, equip you to fight against spiritual battles?

The Final Sip: How can immersing yourself in the Scriptures strengthen you in times of spiritual warfare?

September 4

Strength in God and Not Yourself

"That is why, for Christ's sake, I delight in weaknesses, in insults, in hardships, in persecutions, in difficulties. For when I am weak, then I am strong." (2 Corinthians 12:10, NIV)

Paul isn't celebrating suffering for its own sake, but he recognizes that in his weakest moments, God's power is most evident. As men, we often want to appear strong and capable, but this verse calls us to embrace vulnerability and trust God in every difficulty. It's in those moments of weakness—when we reach the end of ourselves—that God's strength lifts us and carries us through.

 **The Last Ash:** How can you shift your perspective to see difficulties as opportunities?

The Final Sip: What weakness or challenge do you need to surrender to God and trust Him for strength?

September 5

Praying for Victory in Spiritual Warfare

"And pray in the Spirit on all occasions with all kinds of prayers and requests. With this in mind, be alert and always keep on praying for all the Lord's people." (Ephesians 6:18, NIV)

Prayer is a vital component in spiritual warfare. It's not just about asking for help when things get tough, but it's about continuously being in communication with God, staying alert to the enemy's schemes, and interceding for others. Prayer aligns our hearts with God's will, strengthens us in times of trial, and invites God to act on our behalf.

**The Last Ash:** How can prayer be a powerful tool in fighting spiritual battles and claiming victory?

The Final Sip: How does constant communication with God through prayer fortify your spirit and bring peace in the battle?

September 6

Overcoming Fear with Faith

"When I am afraid, I put my trust in you." (Psalm 56:3, NIV)

Fear is one of the enemy's most effective tools to weaken our faith and distract us from God's promises. However, when we choose to trust in God rather than our fears, we allow faith to rise up within us. Faith is the antidote to fear, and it has the power to overcome the uncertainty that may surround us.

The Last Ash: How can focusing on your faith in God help you overcome fear and uncertainty?

The Final Sip: How does trusting in God's faithfulness lead you to walk confidently in His promises, no matter the circumstance?

September 7

God's Power in Your Weakness

"That is why, for Christ's sake, I delight in weaknesses, in insults, in hardships, in persecutions, in difficulties. For when I am weak, then I am strong." (2 Corinthians 12:10, NIV)

The paradox of our weakness becoming strength through God's power is one of the most profound mysteries of the Christian faith. When we acknowledge our weaknesses, we open ourselves to experiencing God's strength in ways we never could if we were relying on our own abilities. In our frailty, His power is made perfect.

The Last Ash: How does experiencing God's power in your weakness strengthen your faith and reliance on Him?

The Final Sip: How can embracing your weakness invite God's strength to be made perfect in your life?

September 8

Battling the Lies of the Enemy

"You belong to your father, the devil, and you want to carry out your father's desires. He was a murderer from the beginning, not holding to the truth, for there is no truth in him. When he lies, he speaks his native language, for he is a liar and the father of lies." (John 8:44, NIV)

The enemy is a master of deception, always attempting to confuse, distort, and lead us into sin with his lies. But when we recognize his lies for what they are and replace them with the truth of God's Word, we gain the strength to stand firm. The truth sets us free, while lies keep us trapped in bondage.

The Last Ash: How can identifying the enemy's lies and replacing them with God's truth help you resist his attacks?

The Final Sip: How does knowing the truth of God's Word give you authority to combat the enemy's deceptions?

September 9

Choosing Truth Over Deception

"Sanctify them by the truth; your word is truth."

(John 17:17, NIV)

In a world full of conflicting messages, God's truth is the one thing we can rely on. Choosing to align our lives with the truth of His Word transforms us, sanctifying us and setting us apart from the world. This decision brings clarity and freedom, allowing us to walk in God's will and His peace.

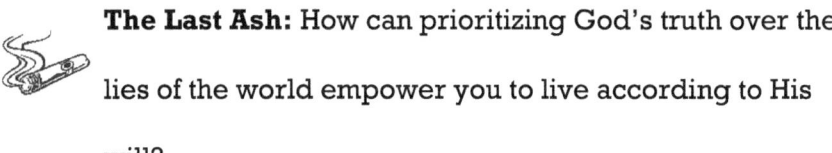

The Last Ash: How can prioritizing God's truth over the lies of the world empower you to live according to His will?

The Final Sip: How does trusting in the truth of God's Word bring clarity and freedom in your life?

September 10

Persevering When the Fight is Long

"I have fought the good fight, I have finished the race, I have kept the faith." (2 Timothy 4:7, NIV)

The journey of faith is not always quick or easy, and sometimes the battle seems endless. But Paul's words remind us that perseverance is key. It's not about winning each individual battle but about staying faithful to the end. When we press on, keeping our eyes on the goal, we honor God and prove our trust in His promises, regardless of how long the fight lasts.

The Last Ash: How can you maintain endurance in the spiritual battle when the fight feels prolonged or discouraging?

The Final Sip: How does staying faithful and focused on God's promises help you finish the race with perseverance?

September 11

Victory in the Name of Jesus

"That at the name of Jesus every knee should bow, in heaven and on earth and under the earth." (Philippians 2:10, NIV)

The name of Jesus holds all authority in heaven and on earth. Every power, whether seen or unseen, is subject to Him. When we face spiritual battles, we can confidently call upon the name of Jesus, knowing that His power is greater than any other force. Victory is assured in His name because He has already won the ultimate victory over sin and death.

The Last Ash: How does invoking the name of Jesus bring victory in every spiritual battle?

The Final Sip: How does knowing that every knee will bow to the name of Jesus encourage you to stand firm in Him?

September 12

Remembering the Battle is the Lord's

"All those gathered here will know that it is not by sword or spear that the Lord saves; for the battle is the Lord's, and he will give all of you into our hands." (1 Samuel 17:47, NIV)

The story of David and Goliath serves as a powerful reminder that the battle belongs to God, not to us. When we face overwhelming challenges, we don't need to rely on our own strength or abilities. Instead, we can trust that God is fighting for us and that He will bring us victory in His way and in His time.

 **The Last Ash:** How can remembering that the battle belongs to the Lord bring peace and confidence in the midst of struggle?

The Final Sip: How does trusting that God fights for you change the way you approach your spiritual challenges?

September 13

Walking by Faith, Not Sight

"For we live by faith, not by sight." (2 Corinthians 5:7, NIV)

Faith allows us to see beyond our circumstances and trust in the unseen promises of God. When we walk by faith, we choose to trust God's character and His Word, rather than being swayed by what we can physically see. Faith anchors us in God's truth, even when the world around us seems uncertain or overwhelming.

 **The Last Ash:** How does walking by faith, not by sight, help you stay anchored in God's promises despite circumstances?

The Final Sip: How can choosing faith over sight bring clarity and peace as you navigate spiritual battles?

September 14

Claiming Your Identity as a Warrior for Christ

"Finally, be strong in the Lord and in his mighty power. Put on the full armor of God, so that you can take your stand against the devil's schemes." (Ephesians 6:10-11, NIV)

As believers, we are called to stand firm and fight against the enemy's attacks. This requires putting on the full armor of God—truth, righteousness, readiness, faith, salvation, and the Word of God. Recognizing our identity as warriors in Christ empowers us to engage in spiritual warfare with confidence, knowing that God equips us for every battle.

The Last Ash: How can embracing your identity as a warrior for Christ empower you to fight the spiritual battle with confidence?

**The Final Sip:** How does putting on the full armor of God equip you to stand strong in your faith?

September 15

The Reward of Endurance

"Blessed is the one who perseveres under trial because, having stood the test, that person will receive the crown of life that the Lord has promised to those who love him." (James 1:12, NIV)

Endurance in the face of trials leads to a promised reward: the crown of life. This reward is not just for enduring hardship, but for enduring with faith and love for God. When we persevere, keeping our eyes fixed on the hope of eternal life, we are strengthened and purified through the process, and we grow in our relationship with God.

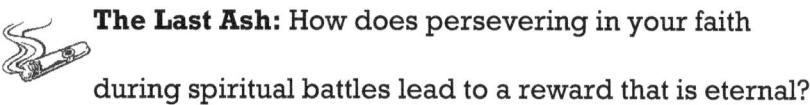

The Last Ash: How does persevering in your faith during spiritual battles lead to a reward that is eternal?

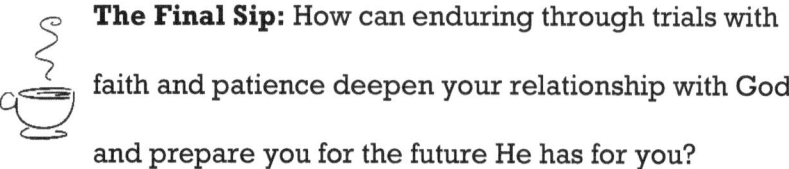

The Final Sip: How can enduring through trials with faith and patience deepen your relationship with God and prepare you for the future He has for you?

September 16

The Battle for Your Mind

"Do not conform to the pattern of this world, but be transformed by the renewing of your mind. Then you will be able to test and approve what God's will is—his good, pleasing and perfect will." (Romans 12:2, NIV)

Spiritual battles often begin in our minds. The world bombards us with lies and distractions, seeking to shape our thoughts. But God calls us to renew our minds through His Word. When we choose to focus on truth, our hearts align with His will, and we gain clarity and wisdom for the battles we face.

**The Last Ash:** How can renewing your mind with God's Word protect you from the lies of the world?

The Final Sip: How does transforming your thoughts allow you to better discern God's will in spiritual warfare?

September 17

Standing Firm in the Truth

"Then you will know the truth, and the truth will set you free." (John 8:32, NIV)

The truth of God's Word is powerful; it exposes lies and sets us free from the enemy's deceit. When we stand firm in the truth, we reject the enemy's lies, no matter how convincing they may seem. Truth brings clarity, freedom, and the power to overcome spiritual attacks.

The Last Ash: How does standing firm in God's truth help you resist the lies of the enemy?

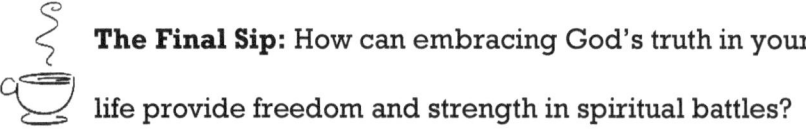

The Final Sip: How can embracing God's truth in your life provide freedom and strength in spiritual battles?

September 18

Guarding Your Heart

"Above all else, guard your heart, for everything you do flows from it." (Proverbs 4:23, NIV)

Our hearts are the wellspring of our thoughts, attitudes, and actions. The enemy often targets our hearts, seeking to sow bitterness, anger, or fear. By guarding our hearts—protecting them from negativity, sin, and distractions—we protect our spiritual health. Keeping our hearts aligned with God allows His peace to reign, even in the midst of spiritual battles.

**The Last Ash:** How can you protect your heart from the influence of fear, anger, and bitterness in spiritual warfare?

The Final Sip: How does guarding your heart allow you to walk in peace and victory during times of struggle?

September 19

The Power of Praise in Battle

"I will extol the Lord at all times; his praise will always be on my lips." (Psalm 34:1, NIV)

Praise is a weapon in spiritual warfare. When we praise God, we shift our focus from the battle to His greatness and power. Praise magnifies God, reminding us that He is bigger than any obstacle. It also invites God's presence into our circumstances, bringing peace and victory in the midst of spiritual struggles.

 **The Last Ash:** How does praising God during spiritual battles remind you of His sovereignty and power?

The Final Sip: How can making praise a consistent part of your life strengthen your resolve in spiritual warfare?

September 20

Trusting God in the Storm

"He got up, rebuked the wind and said to the waves, 'Quiet! Be still!' Then the wind died down and it was completely calm." (Mark 4:39, NIV)

The storms of life can be overwhelming, but Jesus has the authority to calm them. When we face trials, we may feel like we're sinking, but Jesus is present with us. By trusting in His power, we can find peace, even when the storms rage. Jesus's command to the storm is a reminder that He has control over every situation we face.

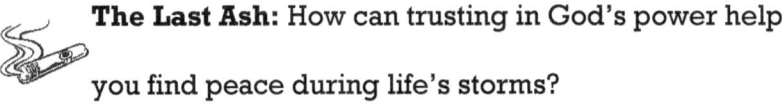
The Last Ash: How can trusting in God's power help you find peace during life's storms?

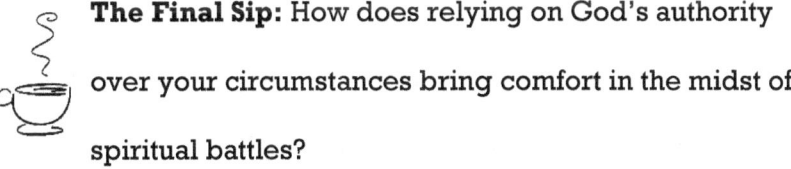
The Final Sip: How does relying on God's authority over your circumstances bring comfort in the midst of spiritual battles?

September 21

Equipped for Battle

"'No weapon forged against you will prevail, and you will refute every tongue that accuses you. This is the heritage of the servants of the Lord, and this is their vindication from me,' declares the Lord." (Isaiah 54:17, NIV)

God equips His servants with everything needed to overcome the enemy. No weapon formed against us will prosper when we are in Christ. This verse reminds us of the spiritual armor that protects us, and the power of God's vindication. When we walk in His strength, we are not only equipped to fight, but guaranteed victory.

The Last Ash: How does knowing that no weapon formed against you will prevail give you confidence in battle?

The Final Sip: How can trusting in God's protection and vindication strengthen you in spiritual warfare?

September 22

Overcoming Temptation with God's Help

"No temptation has overtaken you except what is common to mankind. And God is faithful; he will not let you be tempted beyond what you can bear. But when you are tempted, he will also provide a way out so that you can endure it."
(1 Corinthians 10:13, NIV)

Temptation is a common spiritual struggle, but God promises to provide a way out. His faithfulness ensures that we are not alone in our fight against temptation. We can trust that He will provide the strength and escape routes we need to overcome the enemy's attempts to lead us astray.

 **The Last Ash:** How does knowing that God provides a way out of temptation strengthen your resolve to resist?

The Final Sip: How can trusting in God's faithfulness help you persevere through moments of temptation?

September 23

The Importance of Spiritual Community

"And let us consider how we may spur one another on toward love and good deeds, not giving up meeting together, as some are in the habit of doing, but encouraging one another—and all the more as you see the Day approaching."
(Hebrews 10:24-25, NIV)

Spiritual battles are not meant to be fought alone. God has designed us to be in community with other believers, supporting and encouraging each other. When we meet together and spur one another on, we grow stronger in our faith and are better equipped to face the enemy's attacks.

The Last Ash: How can being part of a spiritual community encourage you in the midst of battle?

The Final Sip: How does surrounding yourself with other believers strengthen your resolve in spiritual warfare?

September 24

Rest in God's Strength

"Come to me, all you who are weary and burdened, and I will give you rest." (Matthew 11:28, NIV)

Spiritual warfare can be exhausting, but Jesus invites us to find rest in Him. When we are weary from the battle, He offers peace and renewal. Trusting in God's strength allows us to lay down our burdens and find the rest we need to continue the fight.

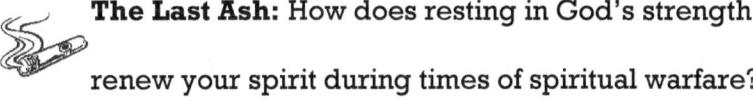 **The Last Ash:** How does resting in God's strength renew your spirit during times of spiritual warfare?

 **The Final Sip:** How can taking time to rest in God's presence help you regain the energy to face future battles?

September 25

Praying with Authority

"Truly I tell you, whatever you bind on earth will be bound in heaven, and whatever you loose on earth will be loosed in heaven." (Matthew 18:18, NIV)

God has given us authority through prayer. When we pray with faith, we tap into the spiritual authority we have in Christ. This verse reminds us that our prayers have power to bind and loose, to declare victory over the enemy and claim God's promises.

The Last Ash: How can understanding the authority you have in Christ empower your prayers in spiritual battles?

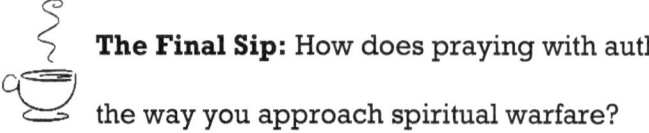
The Final Sip: How does praying with authority change the way you approach spiritual warfare?

September 26

Embracing God's Peace

"Peace I leave with you; my peace I give you. I do not give to you as the world gives. Do not let your hearts be troubled and do not be afraid." (John 14:27, NIV)

In the midst of spiritual warfare, we often experience anxiety and fear. But Jesus offers a peace that surpasses understanding. His peace is not like the world's, which is fleeting, but a deep, abiding peace that guards our hearts. When we embrace God's peace, we can stand firm in the battle, knowing He is with us.

 The Last Ash: How can embracing God's peace calm your heart during spiritual battles?

 **The Final Sip:** How does trusting in God's peace allow you to walk fearlessly in the face of challenges?

September 27

The Battle is Won in Prayer

"The prayer of a righteous person is powerful and effective." (James 5:16, NIV)

Prayer is one of the most powerful weapons we have in spiritual warfare. It connects us with God's power and authority, allowing us to combat the enemy with strength. When we pray with faith, we tap into God's will and bring heaven's resources to bear on earthly situations.

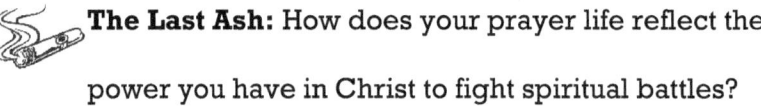**The Last Ash:** How does your prayer life reflect the power you have in Christ to fight spiritual battles?

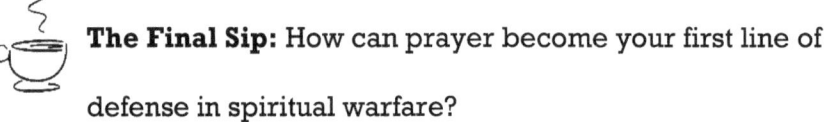**The Final Sip:** How can prayer become your first line of defense in spiritual warfare?

September 28

Victory Through Jesus

"But thanks be to God! He gives us the victory through our Lord Jesus Christ." (1 Corinthians 15:57, NIV)

Our victory in spiritual battles is not based on our own strength, but on Jesus's victory on the cross. Through His death and resurrection, He triumphed over sin, death, and the enemy. When we stand in His victory, we fight from a place of assurance and hope, knowing that the battle has already been won.

The Last Ash: How does remembering Jesus's victory on the cross give you strength in your spiritual battles?

The Final Sip: How can focusing on Jesus's victory empower you in your own spiritual warfare?

September 29

Persevering in the Fight

"Let us not become weary in doing good, for at the proper time we will reap a harvest if we do not give up." (Galatians 6:9, NIV)

Perseverance is key in spiritual warfare. The enemy wants us to give up, to grow weary and faint-hearted. But God promises that if we keep pressing forward in faith, we will reap a harvest of blessings. By staying strong in Him, we can overcome any obstacle the enemy places in our path.

The Last Ash: How can persevering in faith ensure victory over the spiritual battles you face?

The Final Sip: How does remaining steadfast in God's promises help you endure in spiritual warfare?

September 30

The Strength of God's Presence

"Even though I walk through the darkest valley, I will fear no evil, for you are with me; your rod and your staff, they comfort me." (Psalm 23:4, NIV)

In our darkest moments, God's presence is our greatest comfort. When we face spiritual battles that feel overwhelming, we are never alone. His rod and staff guide and protect us, bringing us comfort and peace. With God by our side, we can fear no evil, for He is the strength that sustains us.

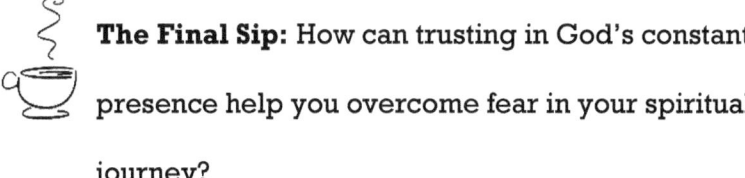

The Last Ash: How does God's presence give you courage in times of spiritual battle?

The Final Sip: How can trusting in God's constant presence help you overcome fear in your spiritual journey?

October

Building Godly Relationships

Who you surround yourself with matters.

This month we will examine our closest circles of influence.

October 1

Loving Others as Christ Loved You

"A new command I give you: Love one another. As I have loved you, so you must love one another." (John 13:34, NIV)

Jesus calls us to love others with the same sacrificial love that He showed us. This kind of love isn't conditional or based on how others treat us, but is modeled after Christ's selfless actions. His love empowers us to love those around us in ways that reflect His heart and bring healing to relationships.

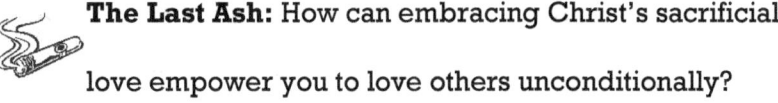

The Last Ash: How can embracing Christ's sacrificial love empower you to love others unconditionally?

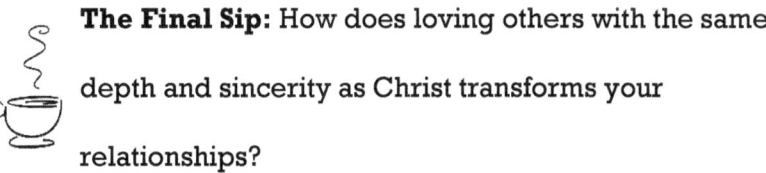

The Final Sip: How does loving others with the same depth and sincerity as Christ transforms your relationships?

October 2

Walking with Friends Who Strengthen Your Faith

"As iron sharpens iron, so one person sharpens another." (Proverbs 27:17, NIV)

Relationships with godly friends are crucial for our spiritual growth. They help us stay sharp in our faith, offer wisdom, and hold us accountable. When we walk alongside those who strengthen our relationship with God, we are encouraged and motivated to pursue Him more passionately.

The Last Ash: How can surrounding yourself with godly friends impact your spiritual growth and walk with God?

The Final Sip: How do relationships with those who encourage your faith help you grow stronger in your relationship with God?

October 3

Forgiving When It's Hard

"For if you forgive other people when they sin against you, your heavenly Father will also forgive you. But if you do not forgive others their sins, your Father will not forgive your sins." (Matthew 6:14-15, NIV)

Forgiveness is not always easy, but it is essential for our own healing and freedom. When we forgive, we reflect the forgiveness that God has shown us, offering grace and mercy in the same way. Choosing to forgive releases bitterness and restores relationships.

The Last Ash: How does forgiving others, especially when it's difficult, reflect Christ's forgiveness toward you?

The Final Sip: How can choosing forgiveness lead to healing and peace in your heart and relationships?

October 4

Speaking Truth in Love

"Instead, speaking the truth in love, we will grow to become in every respect the mature body of him who is the head, that is, Christ." (Ephesians 4:15, NIV)

Truth spoken in love is essential for building healthy relationships. It allows us to be honest while maintaining compassion and kindness. When we share truth with others, we do so in a way that builds them up rather than tearing them down, fostering trust and growth.

The Last Ash: How can speaking the truth in love help you maintain healthy, godly relationships?

The Final Sip: How does balancing truth and love strengthen your ability to share difficult truths with others?

October 5

Serving Others Without Expectation

"For even the Son of Man did not come to be served, but to serve, and to give his life as a ransom for many."
(Mark 10:45, NIV)

Jesus demonstrated the ultimate example of selfless service. By giving His life, He showed us that true greatness is found in serving others without expecting anything in return. Serving others reflects His character and helps to build deeper, more meaningful relationships.

 **The Last Ash:** How can serving others selflessly, as Christ did, foster stronger relationships and reflect His character?

The Final Sip: How does serving without expecting anything in return allow you to experience the joy of giving?

October 6

Patience in Conflict

"A gentle answer turns away wrath, but a harsh word stirs up anger." (Proverbs 15:1, NIV)

In moments of conflict, our words and actions can either escalate or de-escalate the situation. Choosing patience and a gentle response helps to calm the situation and opens the door for understanding. By reflecting Christ's patience in conflict, we can bring peace to strained relationships.

 **The Last Ash:** How can choosing patience in moments of conflict help de-escalate tension and bring about understanding?

The Final Sip: How does responding gently in conflict reflect Christ's love and bring peace to relationships?

October 7

Restoring Broken Relationships

"All this is from God, who reconciled us to himself through Christ and gave us the ministry of reconciliation."
(2 Corinthians 5:18, NIV)

God has called us to the ministry of reconciliation, helping to restore relationships that have been broken. Just as Christ reconciled us to God, we are called to mend relationships with others. Embracing reconciliation requires humility and a willingness to make things right for the sake of peace.

The Last Ash: How does God call us to be agents of reconciliation in relationships that have been fractured?

The Final Sip: How can embracing the ministry of reconciliation help restore and strengthen relationships that have been broken?

October 8

Honoring Your Wife as Christ Honors the Church

"Husbands, in the same way be considerate as you live with your wives, and treat them with respect as the weaker partner and as heirs with you of the gracious gift of life, so that nothing will hinder your prayers." (1 Peter 3:7, NIV)

A husband's role is to love and honor his wife, just as Christ honors the Church. This means showing respect, patience, and care in the relationship. When a husband values and cherishes his wife, it strengthens the marriage and allows both partners to grow together in faith.

The Last Ash: How does honoring your spouse with the same love and care that Christ shows the Church strengthen your marriage?

The Final Sip: How can serving and cherishing your wife help cultivate a Christ-centered relationship?

October 9

The Importance of Brotherhood in Faith

"Two are better than one, because they have a good return for their labor: If either of them falls down, one can help the other up. But pity anyone who falls and has no one to help them up." (Ecclesiastes 4:9-10, NIV)

Strong, supportive relationships are vital in our faith journey. When we walk with others who encourage and challenge us, we grow stronger spiritually. Brotherhood in faith provides mutual support, lifting each other up in times of weakness and celebrating victories together.

The Last Ash: How does building strong bonds with brothers and sisters in Christ offer support and encouragement in your spiritual journey?

The Final Sip: How does walking together in faith with others help you overcome challenges and grow spiritually?

October 10

Leading by Example in Relationships

"Don't let anyone look down on you because you are young, but set an example for the believers in speech, in conduct, in love, in faith and in purity." (1 Timothy 4:12, NIV)

Our actions speak louder than words. When we lead by example in our relationships, we reflect the character of Christ. Through our speech, conduct, and love, we can inspire others to follow Christ's example, showing that leadership comes through humility and living out the truth.

 **The Last Ash:** How does leading by example in your relationships reflect Christ's character and guide others?

The Final Sip: How can living a life of integrity and love inspire others to follow Christ's example?

October 11

Speaking Life into Others

"The tongue has the power of life and death, and those who love it will eat its fruit." (Proverbs 18:21, NIV)

Our words have immense power. When we speak life into others, we build them up and encourage them to walk in the fullness of God's promises. Words can heal, uplift, and inspire—just as Christ's words bring life to those who hear them.

The Last Ash: How does speaking life and encouragement into others uplift and strengthen them in their faith?

The Final Sip: How can your words reflect the life-giving power of God and positively impact those around you?

October 12

Avoiding Gossip and Slander

"A perverse person stirs up conflict, and a gossip separates close friends." (Proverbs 16:28, NIV)

Gossip and slander create division and break trust in relationships. Instead, we are called to speak the truth in love and seek unity. By avoiding harmful speech, we foster a peaceful, respectful environment where relationships can thrive.

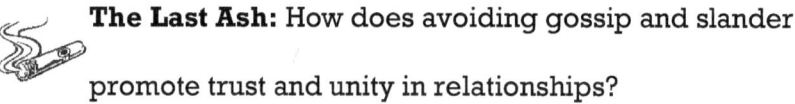
The Last Ash: How does avoiding gossip and slander promote trust and unity in relationships?

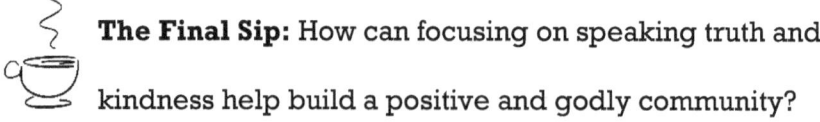
The Final Sip: How can focusing on speaking truth and kindness help build a positive and godly community?

October 13

Reconciling After Hurt

"Therefore, if you are offering your gift at the altar and there remember that your brother or sister has something against you, leave your gift there in front of the altar. First go and be reconciled to them; then come and offer your gift."
(Matthew 5:23-24, NIV)

Reconciliation is crucial for healing. When there is conflict or hurt, God calls us to make things right before offering our worship. Seeking peace and unity restores relationships and honors God's desire for harmony among His people.

The Last Ash: How can seeking reconciliation after hurt or offense bring healing and restore unity?

The Final Sip: How does prioritizing peace and reconciliation honor God and strengthen your relationships?

October 14

Choosing to Love, Even When It's Difficult

"Love is patient, love is kind. It does not envy, it does not boast, it is not proud. It does not dishonor others, it is not self-seeking, it is not easily angered, it keeps no record of wrongs. Love does not delight in evil but rejoices with the truth. It always protects, always trusts, always hopes, always perseveres."

(1 Corinthians 13:4-7, NIV)

Love is a choice, and often it's a choice we must make even in difficult circumstances. The love that Paul describes in 1 Corinthians is unconditional, sacrificial, and constant. When we choose to love in this way, we reflect Christ's love for us and deepen our relationships.

The Last Ash: How can choosing to love unconditionally, despite challenges, reflect the love of Christ in your relationships?

The Final Sip: How does love, even in difficult circumstances, grow and deepen relationships, showing God's transformative power?

October 15

The Joy of Serving Together

"Then make my joy complete by being like-minded, having the same love, being one in spirit and of one mind."
(Philippians 2:2, NIV)

There is great joy in serving together with others who share the same love for Christ. When we unite in purpose and serve one another, we reflect the unity and love of the body of Christ. Working together brings fulfillment, strengthens relationships, and glorifies God.

The Last Ash: How does serving together in unity with others bring joy and strengthen the body of Christ?

The Final Sip: How can shared service and collaboration deepen bonds and create a sense of purpose in your relationships with others?

October 16

The Power of Earnest Prayer

"Elijah was a human being, even as we are. He prayed earnestly that it would not rain, and it did not rain on the land for three and a half years." (James 5:17, NIV)

Elijah's prayers had incredible impact—not because of who he was, but because of his faith and persistence in seeking God. This verse reminds men that prayer is a powerful tool available to all of us, not just spiritual leaders or biblical figures. When we pray with faith and sincerity, God hears and responds. We are called to pray boldly, trusting that God can work through us in extraordinary ways.

The Last Ash: How can you make prayer a more consistent and powerful part of your daily life?

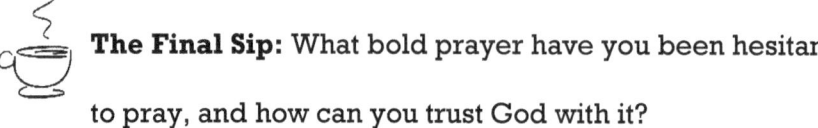

The Final Sip: What bold prayer have you been hesitant to pray, and how can you trust God with it?

October 17

Encouraging One Another in Faith

"Therefore encourage one another and build each other up, just as in fact you are doing." (1 Thessalonians 5:11, NIV)

Encouragement is essential in helping others grow in their faith. A word of encouragement can uplift someone who is struggling, remind them of God's promises, and strengthen their resolve. In community, we are called to build one another up, creating a culture of support and hope.

 **The Last Ash:** How can you be more intentional about encouraging those around you in their faith journey?

The Final Sip: How does offering encouragement help foster stronger and more resilient relationships?

October 18

Bearing One Another's Burdens

"Carry each other's burdens, and in this way you will fulfill the law of Christ." (Galatians 6:2, NIV)

Jesus taught us to bear one another's burdens—offering support in times of difficulty and sharing in each other's struggles. This act of compassion shows the love of Christ and deepens relationships, creating a bond of mutual care and understanding.

The Last Ash: How can you support others by carrying their burdens, both physically and emotionally?

The Final Sip: How does bearing someone else's burdens reflect Christ's love for you and strengthen your relationships?

October 19

The Importance of Listening Well

"My dear brothers and sisters, take note of this: Everyone should be quick to listen, slow to speak and slow to become angry." (James 1:19, NIV)

Listening is an act of love and respect. When we listen well, we show others that we value them, their experiences, and their perspectives. Listening without interrupting or making judgments helps build trust and allows relationships to deepen.

 **The Last Ash:** How does truly listening to others foster deeper connection and understanding?

The Final Sip: How can you practice active listening in your relationships to strengthen communication and trust?

October 20

Honoring Parents and Elders

"Honor your father and mother—which is the first commandment with a promise—so that it may go well with you and that you may enjoy long life on the earth."
(Ephesians 6:2-3, NIV)

Honoring our parents and elders is a commandment that brings blessings. It shows gratitude for the wisdom, sacrifices, and love they have shared with us. By respecting and honoring those who have gone before us, we cultivate deeper relationships and a heart of humility.

The Last Ash: How can honoring your parents and elders impact your life and strengthen familial relationships?

The Final Sip: How does showing respect to those who have nurtured and guided you honor God's commands and bring blessings?

October 21

Living in Peace with Others

"If it is possible, as far as it depends on you, live at peace with everyone." (Romans 12:18, NIV)

Living in peace with others requires intentionality, especially when there are conflicts. We cannot always control how others respond, but we can control our own actions. Striving for peace, offering forgiveness, and seeking reconciliation are key to cultivating healthy relationships.

 **The Last Ash:** How can you actively pursue peace in your relationships, even when it's difficult?

The Final Sip: How does living in peace with others create an environment where love and understanding can thrive?

October 22

Growing in Patience with Others

"Therefore, as God's chosen people, holy and dearly loved, clothe yourselves with compassion, kindness, humility, gentleness and patience. Bear with each other and forgive one another if any of you has a grievance against someone. Forgive as the Lord forgave you." (Colossians 3:12-13, NIV)

Patience is a virtue that reflects God's character. When we bear with one another and show patience, we mirror His long-suffering love. Relationships thrive when we choose patience over frustration, gentleness over harshness, and forgiveness over resentment.

The Last Ash: How can practicing patience in your relationships lead to greater understanding and peace?

The Final Sip: How does extending patience to others reflect God's love for you and help build stronger relationships?

October 23

Being Transparent in Relationships

"But he said to me, 'My grace is sufficient for you, for my power is made perfect in weakness.' Therefore I will boast all the more gladly of my weaknesses, so that the power of Christ may rest upon me." (2 Corinthians 12:9, NIV)

Vulnerability and transparency allow for authentic connections. When we are open about our weaknesses, we invite others to do the same, creating a safe environment for growth and healing. God's grace shines through our weaknesses, and in turn, our relationships become stronger and more genuine.

The Last Ash: How can being transparent in your relationships bring deeper connection and mutual understanding?

The Final Sip: How does embracing vulnerability allow Christ's power to work in and through your relationships?

October 24

Being Slow to Anger

"Whoever is patient has great understanding, but one who is quick-tempered displays folly." (Proverbs 14:29, NIV)

Quick tempers can tear down relationships, while patience builds them up. God calls us to slow down, listen, and understand before reacting. Patience shows understanding and wisdom, helping us to respond thoughtfully rather than reacting impulsively.

The Last Ash: How does cultivating patience and being slow to anger help strengthen your relationships and deepen understanding?

The Final Sip: How can practicing self-control and patience create healthier, more peaceful interactions?

October 25

Cherishing Your Spouse

"Husbands, love your wives, just as Christ loved the church and gave himself up for her." (Ephesians 5:25, NIV)

Loving your spouse selflessly and sacrificially, as Christ loves the Church, is the foundation of a godly marriage. This kind of love is unconditional, generous, and always putting the other person's needs first. When both partners love each other in this way, the relationship grows stronger.

 **The Last Ash:** How can sacrificial love for your spouse create a deeper bond and bring glory to God?

The Final Sip: How does reflecting Christ's love in your marriage build a relationship that honors God?

October 26

Forgiving Yourself

"If we confess our sins, he is faithful and just and will forgive us our sins and purify us from all unrighteousness."
(1 John 1:9, NIV)

Forgiveness starts with God, and it is essential to forgive ourselves as He has forgiven us. Holding onto past mistakes only hinders our spiritual and relational growth. When we accept God's forgiveness, we are freed from guilt and shame, allowing us to move forward in grace.

 **The Last Ash:** How does accepting God's forgiveness help you forgive yourself and heal emotionally?

The Final Sip: How can letting go of past mistakes enable you to grow in healthier relationships?

October 27

Building Trust in Relationships

"Trust in the Lord with all your heart and lean not on your own understanding; in all your ways submit to him, and he will make your paths straight." (Proverbs 3:5-6, NIV)

Trust is the foundation of any strong relationship. As we trust in God, we learn to trust others more deeply. Building trust requires consistency, honesty, and vulnerability, but with God's guidance, we can create relationships grounded in trust and security.

 **The Last Ash:** How does trusting in God enable you to build deeper, more trusting relationships with others?

The Final Sip: How can you invest in trust through consistent actions and transparent communication?

October 28

Patience During Challenges

"Be joyful in hope, patient in affliction, faithful in prayer." (Romans 12:12, NIV)

Patience during difficult times allows us to rely on God's strength. Challenges in relationships or life in general can test our faith, but when we remain patient, we grow in perseverance and character. Trusting in God during tough times helps us navigate hardships with grace.

 **The Last Ash:** How can practicing patience in the face of challenges strengthen your faith and relationships?

The Final Sip: How does keeping hope and staying faithful in prayer sustain you through difficulties?

October 29

Being a Peacemaker

"Blessed are the peacemakers, for they will be called children of God." (Matthew 5:9, NIV)

Peacemakers are those who actively seek to resolve conflict and bring unity. They reflect the heart of God, who desires peace and reconciliation. By pursuing peace, we not only mend relationships but also embody the character of Christ in our interactions.

 **The Last Ash:** How can you be a peacemaker in your relationships and community?

The Final Sip: How does seeking peace mirror the heart of God and bring reconciliation?

October 30

Living with Integrity

"Whoever walks in integrity walks securely, but whoever takes crooked paths will be found out." (Proverbs 10:9, NIV)

Integrity is the bedrock of healthy relationships. When we live with honesty and consistency, we create an atmosphere of trust. Integrity allows us to live without fear of exposure or dishonesty, knowing that we are in alignment with God's will.

The Last Ash: How does living with integrity foster trust and security in your relationships?

 **The Final Sip:** How can you build integrity in your daily actions and interactions with others?

October 31

Thanksgiving for Relationships

"Give thanks in all circumstances; for this is God's will for you in Christ Jesus." (1 Thessalonians 5:18, NIV)

Thanksgiving is an attitude that transforms our perspective. Even in difficult times, we are called to give thanks for the relationships we have. Gratitude opens the door to joy, contentment, and deeper connections with others.

 The Last Ash: How can cultivating a spirit of thanksgiving enhance your relationships?

 **The Final Sip:** What relationships are you most thankful for, and how can you express that gratitude today?

November

Living a Significant Life

The challenge is on!

This month we will identify what actually matters and how you can live a life of purpose.

November 1

Discovering God's Plan for Your Life

"For I know the plans I have for you," declares the Lord, "plans to prosper you and not to harm you, plans to give you a hope and a future." (Jeremiah 29:11, NIV)

God has a unique plan for each of our lives, one that brings hope, purpose, and fulfillment. When we trust His plan, even in moments of uncertainty, we find peace knowing that His ultimate goal for us is good.

 **The Last Ash:** How can trusting God's plan for your life bring peace, even when the future seems uncertain?

The Final Sip: How does seeking God's guidance help you understand and fulfill your purpose in life?

November 2

Living for God's Glory

"So whether you eat or drink or whatever you do, do it all for the glory of God." (1 Corinthians 10:31, NIV)

Every part of our lives, no matter how small or routine, can be done for God's glory. When we align our actions with this purpose, we find greater fulfillment in all that we do.

The Last Ash: How can living every moment with the intention to glorify God shift your daily actions and decisions?

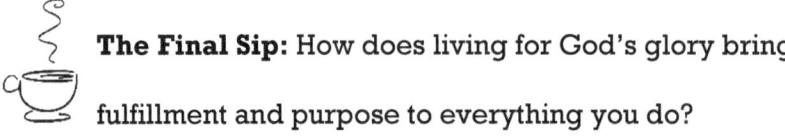

The Final Sip: How does living for God's glory bring fulfillment and purpose to everything you do?

November 3

Faith in the Details

"Whoever can be trusted with very little can also be trusted with much, and whoever is dishonest with very little will also be dishonest with much." (Luke 16:10, NIV)

God values faithfulness in the small, everyday tasks as much as He does in the bigger, more visible responsibilities. Our faithfulness in the little things prepares us for greater opportunities and blessings.

 **The Last Ash:** How can being faithful in small things prepare you for greater responsibilities and blessings?

The Final Sip: How does God use your faithfulness in everyday tasks to strengthen your relationship with Him?

November 4

Pursuing God's Kingdom First

"But seek first his kingdom and his righteousness, and all these things will be given to you as well." (Matthew 6:33, NIV)

When we prioritize God's kingdom and His will, He promises to provide for our needs. This perspective shifts how we view success and redirects our focus toward eternal goals.

 **The Last Ash:** How does prioritizing God's kingdom impact your perspective on life and priorities?

The Final Sip: How can putting God's kingdom first change the way you view success and purpose?

November 5

Running Your Race with Endurance

"Therefore, since we are surrounded by such a great cloud of witnesses, let us throw off everything that hinders and the sin that so easily entangles. And let us run with perseverance the race marked out for us, fixing our eyes on Jesus, the pioneer and perfecter of faith." (Hebrews 12:1-2, NIV)

Life's journey is often compared to a race that requires endurance. By focusing on Jesus, the ultimate example, we gain the strength to persevere through life's challenges.

The Last Ash: How can you stay focused on your race with perseverance, even through challenges and distractions?

The Final Sip: How does keeping your eyes on Jesus give you the strength to endure in life's race?

November 6

Making the Most of Every Opportunity

"Be wise in the way you act toward outsiders; make the most of every opportunity. Let your conversation be always full of grace, seasoned with salt, so that you may know how to answer everyone." (Colossians 4:5-6, NIV)

Every moment is an opportunity to reflect God's grace and truth. Being intentional with how we spend our time can align our daily actions with His divine purposes.

 **The Last Ash:** How can being intentional with every opportunity bring God's purpose into your daily life?

The Final Sip: How does being mindful of time and opportunities help you live more purposefully?

November 7

Leaving a Legacy of Faith

"I have fought the good fight, I have finished the race, I have kept the faith. Now there is in store for me the crown of righteousness, which the Lord, the righteous Judge, will award to me on that day—and not only to me, but also to all who have longed for his appearing." (2 Timothy 4:7-8, NIV)

Living with purpose today sets the foundation for a legacy of faith that will continue to impact others for generations. Our faithful actions, fueled by love for Christ, leave an eternal imprint.

The Last Ash: How does living with purpose today help you leave a lasting legacy of faith for future generations?

The Final Sip: How can focusing on eternity guide you in leaving a legacy that honors God?

November 8

The Purpose of Your Work

"Whatever you do, work at it with all your heart, as working for the Lord, not for human masters, since you know that you will receive an inheritance from the Lord as a reward. It is the Lord Christ you are serving." (Colossians 3:23-24, NIV)

No matter what our occupation may be, we are called to work with excellence as if serving God directly. This transforms every task into an opportunity to glorify Him.

The Last Ash: How can you view your work as a service to God, regardless of your career or occupation?

The Final Sip: How does working with all your heart, as if for the Lord, give purpose to your daily tasks?

November 9

Being Salt and Light in the World

"You are the salt of the earth... You are the light of the world. A town built on a hill cannot be hidden. Neither do people light a lamp and put it under a bowl. Instead, they put it on its stand, and it gives light to everyone in the house."
(Matthew 5:13-16, NIV)

As followers of Christ, we are called to be the salt and light of the world, living in such a way that others are drawn to Him. Our actions and words reflect His love and truth to a world in need.

 The Last Ash: How can you shine Christ's light and flavor the world with His truth through your actions?

 **The Final Sip:** How does being a witness for Christ in the world bring purpose to your daily life?

November 10

Surrendering Your Will to God's Purpose

"Therefore, I urge you, brothers and sisters, in view of God's mercy, to offer your bodies as a living sacrifice, holy and pleasing to God—this is your true and proper worship." (Romans 12:1, NIV)

Surrendering our will to God's purpose means living intentionally for Him. As we yield to His guidance, He transforms our hearts and minds, aligning us more fully with His plan for our lives.

The Last Ash: How can surrendering your will to God's purpose bring peace and joy, even in difficult circumstances?

The Final Sip: How does submitting to God's perfect will help you live with greater clarity and purpose?

November 11

Finding Fulfillment in Serving Others

"You, my brothers and sisters, were called to be free. But do not use your freedom to indulge the flesh; rather, serve one another humbly in love." (Galatians 5:13, NIV)

Serving others is not just about meeting their needs—it's about loving them selflessly, as Christ has loved us. Serving brings true fulfillment because it aligns us with God's heart for others.

 **The Last Ash:** How does serving others fulfill your purpose and bring joy to your life?

The Final Sip: How can a life of service lead to true satisfaction and deeper relationships with others?

November 12

Using Your Gifts for God's Glory

"Each of you should use whatever gift you have received to serve others, as faithful stewards of God's grace in its various forms." (1 Peter 4:10, NIV)

God has uniquely gifted each of us to serve others. By using our talents for His glory, we fulfill His purpose in our lives and contribute to His kingdom work.

 **The Last Ash:** How can using your unique gifts honor God and benefit others?

The Final Sip: How does stewarding your talents and abilities for God's glory align your life with His purpose?

November 13

Living a Life That Reflects Christ

"For to me, to live is Christ and to die is gain."

(Philippians 1:21, NIV)

When Christ becomes our central focus, every aspect of our life becomes an opportunity to reflect His love and grace. Our purpose is found in living for Him and making His name known in all we do.

 **The Last Ash:** How can living for Christ make every part of your life a reflection of His love and grace?

The Final Sip: How does surrendering your life to Christ transform the way you live, love, and serve?

November 14

Trusting God to Open Doors

"I know your deeds. See, I have placed before you an open door that no one can shut. I know that you have little strength, yet you have kept my word and have not denied my name." (Revelation 3:8, NIV)

God holds the keys to every door in our lives. When we trust His timing and rely on His strength, He opens doors that lead to opportunities we could never have imagined.

 **The Last Ash:** How does trusting in God's timing and plan help you step into new opportunities with confidence?

The Final Sip: How does God's sovereignty over open and closed doors give you peace in life's transitions?

November 15

Building for Eternity, Not for Earth

"Do not store up for yourselves treasures on earth, where moths and vermin destroy, and where thieves break in and steal. But store up for yourselves treasures in heaven, where moths and vermin do not destroy, and where thieves do not break in and steal." (Matthew 6:19-20, NIV)

Earthly possessions are temporary, but the investments we make in God's kingdom will last forever. Our focus should be on building for eternity rather than accumulating temporary treasures.

The Last Ash: How can focusing on eternal rewards instead of earthly possessions shift your perspective on life?

The Final Sip: How does investing in God's kingdom and eternal purposes lead to a life of lasting significance?

November 16

Embracing God's Discipline

"No discipline seems pleasant at the time, but painful. Later on, however, it produces a harvest of righteousness and peace for those who have been trained by it." (Hebrews 12:11, NIV)

Discipline from God may feel uncomfortable, but it's a necessary part of our growth. His loving correction shapes us to be more like Christ, resulting in peace and righteousness.

The Last Ash: How can embracing God's discipline lead to spiritual growth and maturity in your life?

The Final Sip: How does trusting God's process help you respond to discipline with gratitude instead of resistance?

November 17

Learning from Life's Challenges

"Consider it pure joy, my brothers and sisters, whenever you face trials of many kinds, because you know that the testing of your faith produces perseverance. Let perseverance finish its work so that you may be mature and complete, not lacking anything." (James 1:2-4, NIV)

Challenges are a natural part of life, but they are also opportunities for growth. When we approach them with faith, they become the training ground for perseverance and spiritual maturity.

The Last Ash: How can seeing trials as opportunities for growth help you navigate life's challenges with a different mindset?

The Final Sip: How does perseverance developed through trials help you become more complete in your faith?

November 18

The Power of Forgiveness

"Be kind and compassionate to one another, forgiving each other, just as in Christ God forgave you." (Ephesians 4:32, NIV)

Forgiveness is a powerful act of grace, and when we forgive others, we reflect the love and mercy that God has shown us. Letting go of resentment frees us to walk in peace and freedom.

 **The Last Ash:** How can forgiving others, even when it's difficult, bring freedom and peace to your heart?

The Final Sip: How does forgiving others reflect the grace God has shown you?

November 19

Living in Obedience to God's Word

"If you love me, keep my commands." (John 14:15, NIV)

Obedience to God's Word is an expression of our love for Him. It's through obedience that we experience His presence and align ourselves with His perfect will.

 **The Last Ash:** How does living in obedience to God's commands reflect your love for Him?

The Final Sip: How can obedience lead to a deeper relationship with God?

November 20

Persevering in Prayer

"Pray continually." (1 Thessalonians 5:17, NIV)

Prayer is not just a one-time event, but a continual conversation with God. It's through consistent prayer that we grow closer to Him, find guidance, and gain strength for the challenges ahead.

The Last Ash: How does making prayer a regular part of your life strengthen your relationship with God?

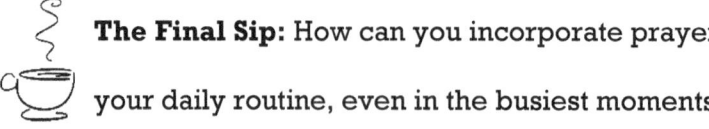

The Final Sip: How can you incorporate prayer into your daily routine, even in the busiest moments?

November 21

The Blessings of Generosity

"In everything I did, I showed you that by this kind of hard work we must help the weak, remembering the words the Lord Jesus himself said: 'It is more blessed to give than to receive.'"
(Acts 20:35, NIV)

Generosity is a reflection of God's heart. When we give, whether through time, resources, or love, we not only bless others but also experience God's blessings in return.

 **The Last Ash:** How does living a generous life open your heart to experience God's blessings?

The Final Sip: How can practicing generosity impact both your life and the lives of those around you?

November 22

Strength through Grace

"You then, my son, be strong in the grace that is in Christ Jesus." (2 Timothy 2:1, NIV)

This grace empowers and sustains us in every challenge. For men striving to lead, endure hardship, and remain faithful, this verse is a reminder that our strength is rooted in God's unmerited favor, not in our own efforts. True strength comes from acknowledging our dependence on Christ and allowing His grace to guide and uphold us in every situation.

The Last Ash: Where in your life do you need to rely more on God's grace for strength?

The Final Sip: How can God's grace help you face the challenges and responsibilities?

November 23

Living with Eternal Perspective

"For God so loved the world that he gave his one and only Son, that whoever believes in him shall not perish but have eternal life." (John 3:16, NIV)

God's love isn't passive; it's sacrificial. He gave His Son so we could have eternal life, not because we earned it but because of His grace. For men seeking meaning and purpose, this verse is a call to receive and embrace that love, trusting in Jesus for salvation. It's also a challenge to reflect that love to others, living lives marked by grace, sacrifice, and faith in God's promises.

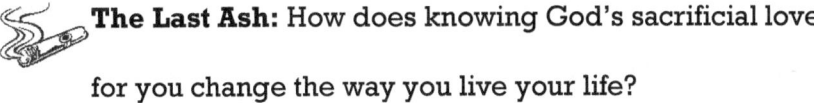**The Last Ash:** How does knowing God's sacrificial love for you change the way you live your life?

**The Final Sip:** What steps can you take to reflect God's love to those around you?

November 24

Living a Life of Integrity

"Whoever walks in integrity walks securely, but whoever takes crooked paths will be found out." (Proverbs 10:9, NIV)

Integrity is the foundation of a trustworthy life. Living with honesty and righteousness gives us confidence and peace, knowing that our actions are aligned with God's standards.

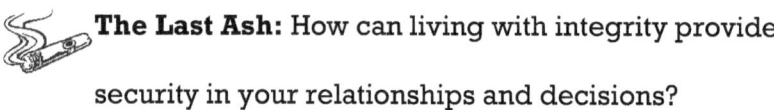 **The Last Ash:** How can living with integrity provide security in your relationships and decisions?

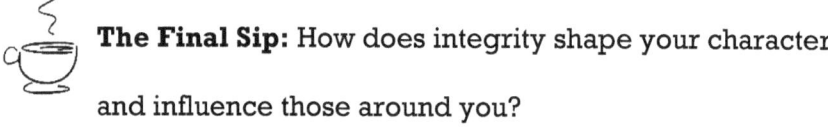 **The Final Sip:** How does integrity shape your character and influence those around you?

November 25

God's Timing is Perfect

"He has made everything beautiful in its time. He has also set eternity in the human heart; yet no one can fathom what God has done from beginning to end." (Ecclesiastes 3:11, NIV)

God's timing is always perfect, even when we don't understand it. Trusting that He has a plan for every moment helps us live with patience and confidence, knowing that He is in control.

 **The Last Ash:** How does trusting in God's perfect timing help you live with patience and faith?

The Final Sip: How can remembering that God has set eternity in your heart encourage you to trust His plans for your life?

November 26

Choosing Joy in All Circumstances

"Rejoice in the Lord always. I will say it again: Rejoice!" (Philippians 4:4, NIV)

Joy is not based on circumstances but on our relationship with God. When we choose to rejoice in Him, we find peace and strength that transcends our situations.

The Last Ash: How can you choose joy in all circumstances, even in the midst of challenges?

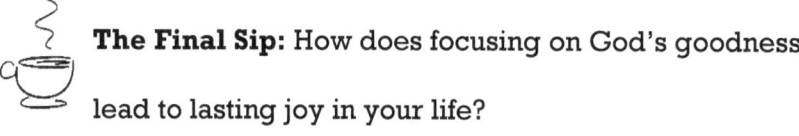

The Final Sip: How does focusing on God's goodness lead to lasting joy in your life?

November 27

Trusting God's Provision

"And my God will meet all your needs according to the riches of his glory in Christ Jesus." (Philippians 4:19, NIV)

God is faithful to provide for all our needs. Trusting in His provision allows us to live with confidence, knowing that He will supply everything we need to fulfill His purpose for our lives.

 **The Last Ash:** How does trusting in God's provision allow you to live with greater peace and confidence?

The Final Sip: How can remembering God's faithfulness to meet your needs strengthen your trust in Him?

November 28

The Blessing of Contentment

"I am not saying this because I am in need, for I have learned to be content whatever the circumstances. I know what it is to be in need, and I know what it is to have plenty. I have learned the secret of being content in any and every situation..."
(Philippians 4:11-12, NIV)

Contentment is not about circumstances but about having a heart that trusts God. By focusing on His provision and sovereignty, we can find peace in every season of life.

The Last Ash: How can contentment in all circumstances help you live with greater peace and purpose?

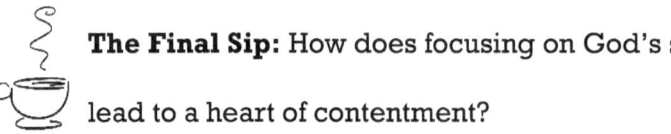

The Final Sip: How does focusing on God's sufficiency lead to a heart of contentment?

November 29

Delighting in God's Presence

"Take delight in the Lord, and he will give you the desires of your heart." (Psalm 37:4, NIV)

It's not a promise to give us everything we want but an invitation to align our desires with His will. When we delight in the Lord—seeking His presence, trusting His plan, and walking in obedience—our hearts begin to reflect His desires. True satisfaction is found not in chasing worldly success but in pursuing God first.

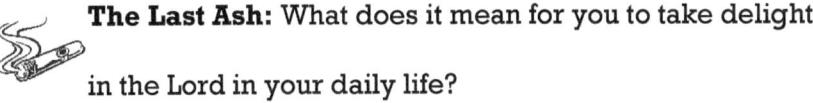

The Last Ash: What does it mean for you to take delight in the Lord in your daily life?

The Final Sip: How has God shaped your desires when you've trusted and sought Him first?

November 30

Celebrating God's Faithfulness

"Because of the Lord's great love we are not consumed, for his compassions never fail. They are new every morning; great is your faithfulness." (Lamentations 3:22-23, NIV)

God's faithfulness is unwavering, and His mercies are renewed each day. As we reflect on His goodness, we are reminded of the incredible love and grace He offers us daily.

The Last Ash: How can celebrating God's faithfulness deepen your gratitude and trust in Him?

The Final Sip: How does reflecting on God's unwavering love and mercy inspire you to live with greater faith?

December

Preparing for Eternity

The reason for the season.

Knowing now what we know, let us be that light, walk the walk, prepared to meet our maker for all eternity.

And pray we may hear His words,

"Well done, good and faithful servant!"

(Matthew 25:23, NIV)

December 1

Fixing Your Eyes on Heaven

"Set your minds on things above, not on earthly things." (Colossians 3:2, NIV)

Setting our minds on things above shifts our focus from the fleeting to the eternal. When we think about heaven, we are reminded of the hope, peace, and purpose that await us. Our daily lives become a reflection of our heavenly priorities, and we live in light of eternity.

 **The Last Ash**: How does setting your heart on heaven shape the way you live and make decisions on earth?

The Final Sip: How does focusing on the eternal promise of heaven give you hope in life's trials?

December 2

Walking in the Hope of Eternal Life

"In the hope of eternal life, which God, who does not lie, promised before the beginning of time." (Titus 1:2, NIV)

The promise of eternal life is not just for the future but should affect how we live today. This hope gives us confidence and perseverance through life's challenges, knowing that the suffering of today is temporary compared to the eternal joy ahead.

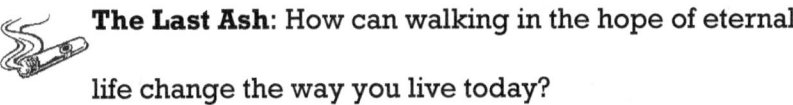 **The Last Ash**: How can walking in the hope of eternal life change the way you live today?

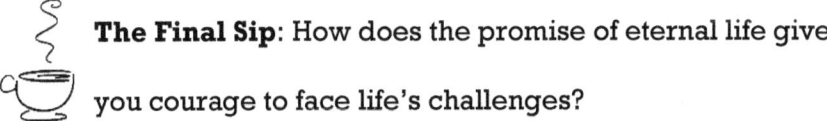 **The Final Sip**: How does the promise of eternal life give you courage to face life's challenges?

December 3

Storing Up Heavenly Treasures

"But store up for yourselves treasures in heaven, where moths and vermin do not destroy, and where thieves do not break in and steal." (Matthew 6:20, NIV)

Earthly treasures are fleeting, but heavenly treasures are eternal. By investing in what pleases God—acts of service, love, and faith—we store up treasures that will last forever. When we shift our focus from worldly accumulation to eternal impact, we align our hearts with God's kingdom.

The Last Ash: How can you lay up treasures in heaven by living for God's kingdom and His purposes?

The Final Sip: How does shifting your focus to heavenly treasures help you live with eternal perspective?

December 4

Keeping an Eternal Perspective

"For our light and momentary troubles are achieving for us an eternal glory that far outweighs them all. So we fix our eyes not on what is seen, but on what is unseen, since what is seen is temporary, but what is unseen is eternal."
(2 Corinthians 4:17-18, NIV)

Our trials and struggles may seem overwhelming in the moment, but when viewed through the lens of eternity, they are temporary. This perspective helps us endure, knowing that every hardship is preparing us for the glory that awaits us.

The Last Ash: How does maintaining an eternal perspective help you endure life's temporary struggles?

The Final Sip: How does remembering that our light and momentary troubles are preparing us for eternal glory impact how you handle trials?

December 5

Anticipating Christ's Return

"For the Lord himself will come down from heaven, with a loud command, with the voice of the archangel and with the trumpet call of God, and the dead in Christ will rise first. After that, we who are still alive and are left will be caught up together with them in the clouds to meet the Lord in the air. And so we will be with the Lord forever." (1 Thessalonians 4:16-17, NIV)

The return of Christ is our ultimate hope. His return will bring victory, resurrection, and eternal life. Living with the anticipation of Christ's return changes how we live today—it encourages us to live faithfully, knowing we are called to be ready at any moment.

The Last Ash: How does eagerly anticipating Christ's return bring hope and purpose to your daily life?

The Final Sip: How does living in light of Christ's return influence your decisions and relationships?

December 6

The Joy of the Resurrection Promise

"Jesus said to her, 'I am the resurrection and the life. The one who believes in me will live, even though they die; and whoever lives by believing in me will never die. Do you believe this?'" (John 11:25-26, NIV)

The resurrection of Jesus gives us the hope of eternal life. For those who believe in Him, death is not the end but a transition into eternal life. This promise of resurrection brings joy, even in the face of death, knowing that we will be with Him forever.

The Last Ash: How does the promise of resurrection bring joy and peace, even in the face of death?

The Final Sip: How can the resurrection hope help you live a life filled with joy and gratitude?

December 7

Living Today as If Christ Comes Tomorrow

"Therefore keep watch, because you do not know on what day your Lord will come." (Matthew 24:42, NIV)

Living with the awareness that Christ could return at any moment keeps us alert and ready. It shapes our priorities, relationships, and actions. If we are prepared for His return, we will be living in a way that honors God and reflects our hope in Him.

**The Last Ash**: How does living with the awareness that Christ may return at any moment shape your actions and priorities?

The Final Sip: How does being ready for Christ's return inspire you to live with urgency and purpose?

December 8

Preparing Your Heart for Eternity

"The world and its desires pass away, but whoever does the will of God lives forever." (1 John 2:17, NIV)

The world offers temporary pleasures and distractions, but they do not last. By focusing on the will of God and eternal life, we prepare our hearts for what truly matters. This commitment to God's will is what secures our place in eternity.

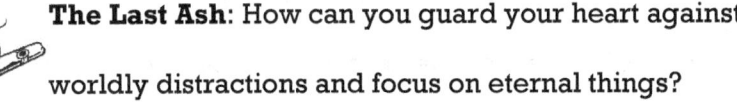 **The Last Ash**: How can you guard your heart against worldly distractions and focus on eternal things?

 **The Final Sip**: How does preparing your heart for eternity bring peace and joy in the present?

December 9

Seeking God's Kingdom Above All Else

"But seek first his kingdom and his righteousness, and all these things will be given to you as well." (Matthew 6:33, NIV)

Prioritizing God's kingdom over everything else transforms our lives. When we seek His righteousness first, everything else falls into place. This kingdom-focused life gives us peace, purpose, and direction in all we do.

The Last Ash: How does prioritizing God's kingdom and His righteousness change your perspective on life?

The Final Sip: How does seeking God's kingdom help you find purpose and peace in every area of life?

December 10

The Crown of Righteousness Awaits You

"Now there is in store for me the crown of righteousness, which the Lord, the righteous Judge, will award to me on that day—and not only to me, but also to all who have longed for his appearing." (2 Timothy 4:8, NIV)

The crown of righteousness represents the reward for those who faithfully live for God's kingdom. The promise of eternal rewards fuels our perseverance. We live not for temporary satisfaction, but for eternal glory with Christ.

The Last Ash: How does knowing there is a crown of righteousness awaiting you motivate you to persevere in faith?

The Final Sip: How does the hope of eternal rewards inspire you to remain faithful and diligent in your walk with God?

December 11

Encouraging One Another About Heaven

"Therefore encourage one another and build each other up, just as in fact you are doing." (1 Thessalonians 5:11, NIV)

Reminding one another of the hope of heaven strengthens our faith and keeps us focused on eternal things. When we encourage each other, we help one another endure the hardships of life with the confidence that our reward in heaven is secure.

The Last Ash: How can you encourage others with the hope of heaven to strengthen their faith?

The Final Sip: How does reminding each other about the eternal promises of God strengthen your community?

December 12

Passing on the Hope of Salvation

"How, then, can they call on the one they have not believed in? And how can they believe in the one of whom they have not heard? And how can they hear without someone preaching to them? And how can anyone preach unless they are sent? As it is written, 'How beautiful are the feet of those who bring good news!'" (Romans 10:14-15, NIV)

The message of salvation is the most important gift we can share. By passing it on, we offer others the hope of eternal life. Our role as messengers helps spread the gospel to those who need to hear and believe in Jesus Christ.

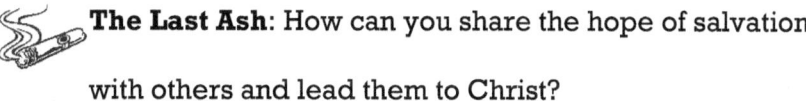**The Last Ash**: How can you share the hope of salvation with others and lead them to Christ?

**The Final Sip**: How does passing on the message of salvation help others find eternal hope and peace?

December 13

Standing Firm Until the End

"But the one who stands firm to the end will be saved."

(Matthew 24:13, NIV)

Faithfulness through trials is key to receiving the reward of eternal life. The promise that those who endure until the end will be saved encourages us to stay strong in the faith, no matter the difficulties we face.

The Last Ash: How can you remain faithful to God and stand firm in your faith, even when life gets tough?

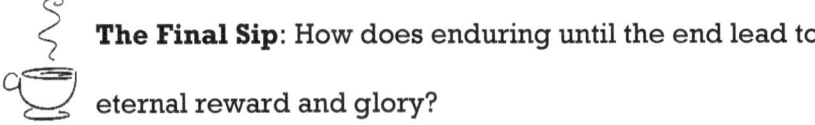

The Final Sip: How does enduring until the end lead to eternal reward and glory?

December 14

Being Ready to Meet the Lord

"Therefore this is what I will do to you, Israel, and because I will do this to you, prepare to meet your God, O Israel."
(Amos 4:12, NIV)

We are called to live in a state of readiness for when we meet the Lord. This readiness involves living in obedience and keeping our hearts aligned with His will. By preparing for this encounter, we remain faithful and focused on our eternal home.

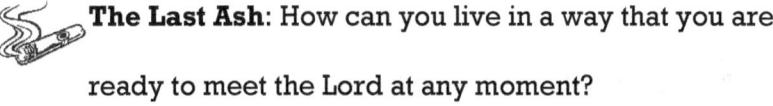 **The Last Ash**: How can you live in a way that you are ready to meet the Lord at any moment?

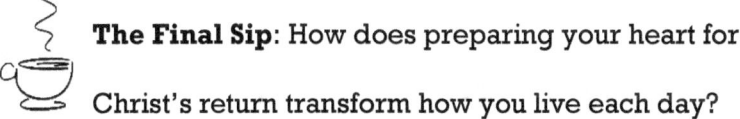 **The Final Sip**: How does preparing your heart for Christ's return transform how you live each day?

December 15

Rejoicing in the Promise of Eternity

"He will wipe every tear from their eyes. There will be no more death or mourning or crying or pain, for the old order of things has passed away." (Revelation 21:4, NIV)

The promise of eternity with God brings ultimate joy and comfort. When we focus on the eternal life He offers, we find peace in the present. All pain, sorrow, and loss will be replaced by the perfect joy of being with Him forever.

 **The Last Ash**: How does the promise of eternity with God bring joy and comfort in your life today?

The Final Sip: How can focusing on the eternal promise of God's presence fill your life with peace and hope?

December 16

Being Born Again

"Look, I am coming soon! My reward is with me, and I will give to each person according to what they have done." (Revelation 22:12, NIV)

Christ's return is certain, and with it comes the reward for our faithfulness. We are reminded that every act of obedience and service counts toward our eternal reward. This should motivate us to live each day with purpose and dedication, knowing that our labor for God is not in vain.

The Last Ash: How does the promise of Christ's return and the rewards awaiting motivate your actions today?

The Final Sip: How does living with the awareness that your works will be rewarded inspire you to be faithful and diligent in your walk with Christ?

December 17

Living as Ambassadors for Christ

"We are therefore Christ's ambassadors, as though God were making his appeal through us. We implore you on Christ's behalf: Be reconciled to God." (2 Corinthians 5:20, NIV)

As ambassadors for Christ, we represent His kingdom on earth. Our lives should reflect His character, His values, and His message of reconciliation. This responsibility is not just a duty but a privilege, as we have been entrusted with the most important mission—inviting others into a relationship with God.

 **The Last Ash**: How can you live as an ambassador for Christ, reflecting His values and sharing His message?

The Final Sip: How does embracing your role as Christ's ambassador change the way you interact with the world?

December 18

Enduring in Faith Until the End

"Blessed is the one who perseveres under trial because, having stood the test, that person will receive the crown of life that the Lord has promised to those who love him." (James 1:12, NIV)

Trials and difficulties are a part of life, but those who persevere through them with faith are promised the crown of life. Endurance in faith refines us and strengthens our relationship with God, and it prepares us for the eternal rewards that await those who remain faithful.

 **The Last Ash**: How can you persevere in faith through life's challenges, trusting that there is a reward for your endurance?

The Final Sip: How does the promise of the crown of life encourage you to remain steadfast in your walk with God?

December 19

The Hope of a New Heaven and New Earth

"Then I saw 'a new heaven and a new earth,' for the first heaven and the first earth had passed away, and there was no longer any sea." (Revelation 21:1, NIV)

The hope of a new heaven and a new earth gives us something to look forward to beyond this life. In God's perfect plan, He will restore and renew all things. This vision of a restored creation gives us peace and encourages us to persevere through the trials of this world, knowing that one day all will be made new.

The Last Ash: How does the promise of a new heaven and earth shape your outlook on the present world?

The Final Sip: How does the hope of God's ultimate restoration give you confidence and peace in your daily life?

December 20

Living as Sons and Daughters of God

"Dear friends, now we are children of God, and what we will be has not yet been made known. But we know that when Christ appears, we shall be like him, for we shall see him as he is." (1 John 3:2, NIV)

As children of God, we have the incredible privilege of being part of His eternal family. The fullness of our future identity will be revealed when Christ appears, and we will be transformed to be like Him. This promise of transformation gives us hope and motivates us to live in the image of Christ today.

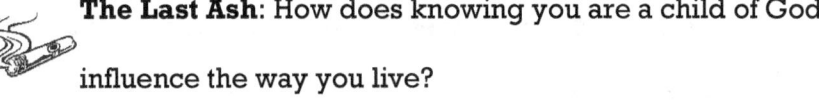 **The Last Ash**: How does knowing you are a child of God influence the way you live?

 **The Final Sip**: How does the promise of becoming like Christ shape your actions and desires in this life?

December 21

The Great Celebration of Heaven

"Let us rejoice and be glad and give him glory! For the wedding of the Lamb has come, and his bride has made herself ready. Fine linen, bright and clean, was given her to wear." (Fine linen stands for the righteous acts of God's holy people.) Then the angel said to me, 'Write this: Blessed are those who are invited to the wedding supper of the Lamb!' And he added, 'These are the true words of God.'" (Revelation 19:7-9, NIV)

The wedding supper of the Lamb is the ultimate celebration, a time when Christ's bride, the Church, is united with Him in eternal joy. This image of celebration reminds us that our faithfulness leads to a future of unimaginable joy and communion with Christ.

The Last Ash: How does the wedding supper of the Lamb influence your view of heaven and eternity?

The Final Sip: How does the promise of eternal celebration with Christ encourage you to persevere in faith today?

December 22

The Hope of the Resurrection

"But our citizenship is in heaven. And we eagerly await a Savior from there, the Lord Jesus Christ, who, by the power that enables him to bring everything under his control, will transform our lowly bodies so that they will be like his glorious body." (Philippians 3:20-21, NIV)

As citizens of heaven, we eagerly await the transformation that will come when Christ returns. Our current bodies are weak and subject to decay, but when Christ comes, He will transform them into glorious bodies like His own. This resurrection gives us hope and strengthens our resolve to live for Him.

The Last Ash: How does the hope of the resurrection and the transformation of your body inspire you to live with eternity in mind?

The Final Sip: How does anticipating the resurrection influence the way you view your present struggles and limitations?

December 23

The Glory of God's Presence

"There will be no more night. They will not need the light of a lamp or the light of the sun, for the Lord God will give them light. And they will reign forever and ever."
(Revelation 22:5, NIV)

In God's eternal kingdom, there will be no darkness—His glory will illuminate everything. This vision of God's presence as the eternal source of light gives us comfort and assurance that in His presence, there will be no more fear, sorrow, or pain.

 **The Last Ash**: How does the thought of living in the eternal light of God's presence bring comfort and hope?

The Final Sip: How does the promise of God's presence forever give you peace and joy in the present moment?

December 24

The Promise of God's Unfailing Love

"Neither height nor depth, nor anything else in all creation, will be able to separate us from the love of God that is in Christ Jesus our Lord." (Romans 8:39, NIV)

God's love for us is unbreakable and eternal. No circumstance, hardship, or fear can separate us from His love. This unshakable promise of God's love gives us confidence as we look to eternity.

The Last Ash: How does the certainty of God's unfailing love give you security and peace?

The Final Sip: How does God's love shape the way you live each day, knowing that nothing can separate you from it?

December 25

Christmas: Celebrating the Birth of Jesus

"Today in the town of David a Savior has been born to you; he is the Messiah, the Lord." (Luke 2:11, NIV)

The birth of Jesus marks the beginning of God's incredible gift of salvation to the world. This gift, given freely, leads us to eternal life through His death and resurrection. Christmas reminds us that our hope for eternity is rooted in the Savior who came to redeem us.

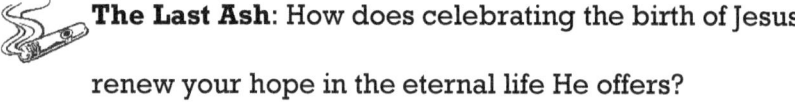**The Last Ash**: How does celebrating the birth of Jesus renew your hope in the eternal life He offers?

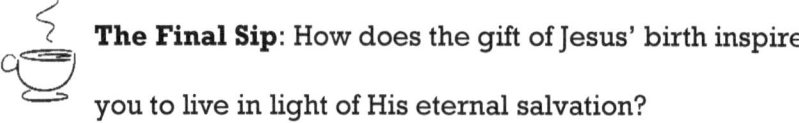**The Final Sip**: How does the gift of Jesus' birth inspire you to live in light of His eternal salvation?

December 26

The Promise of New Life

"Therefore, if anyone is in Christ, the new creation has come: The old has gone, the new is here!" (2 Corinthians 5:17, NIV)

In Christ, we are made new. The old has passed away, and we are given new life, both now and for eternity. This transformation is the beginning of an eternal journey with Christ, one that will continue forever in the presence of God.

The Last Ash: How has your life been transformed by Christ, and how does this new creation affect your outlook on eternity?

The Final Sip: How does the promise of new life in Christ encourage you to live with a fresh perspective on your future with God?

December 27

The Hope of Glory

"To them God has chosen to make known among the Gentiles the glorious riches of this mystery, which is Christ in you, the hope of glory." (Colossians 1:27, NIV)

Christ in us is the hope of glory, the assurance of our future with Him in heaven. This mystery is revealed to all who believe—God's presence with us now is a foretaste of the glory that awaits. This hope encourages us to live for Him now, as we anticipate the glory that will be revealed in us.

 **The Last Ash**: How does the Holy Spirit fill you with hope as you look forward to the glory to come?

The Final Sip: How can you live today with the hope of glory, knowing Christ is in you?

December 28

Living with Eternal Perspective

"So we fix our eyes not on what is seen, but on what is unseen, since what is seen is temporary, but what is unseen is eternal." (2 Corinthians 4:18, NIV)

An eternal perspective helps us to see beyond the temporary struggles and challenges of this life. What we can see is fleeting, but the things that are unseen—the promises of God and His eternal kingdom—are forever. Keeping our eyes fixed on eternity helps us live with purpose and peace, even in the midst of life's uncertainties.

The Last Ash: How can you focus more on the eternal rather than the temporary struggles of life?

The Final Sip: How does living with an eternal perspective impact your daily choices and attitude?

December 29

Enduring Hope in God's Promises

"For everything that was written in the past was written to teach us, so that through the endurance taught in the Scriptures and the encouragement they provide we might have hope."
(Romans 15:4, NIV)

The Bible is full of promises that encourage and strengthen us in our faith. As we meditate on God's Word, we are reminded of His faithfulness and His plan for our lives. This hope enables us to endure through hardships, knowing that God is with us and His promises are sure.

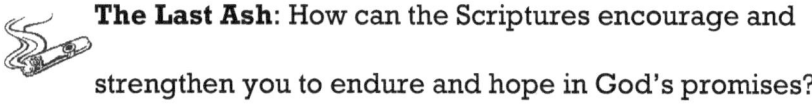

The Last Ash: How can the Scriptures encourage and strengthen you to endure and hope in God's promises?

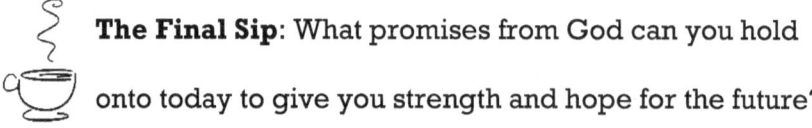

The Final Sip: What promises from God can you hold onto today to give you strength and hope for the future?

December 30

The Gift of Grace

"For it is by grace you have been saved, through faith—and this is not from yourselves, it is the gift of God—not by works, so that no one can boast." (Ephesians 2:8-9, NIV)

Grace is God's unmerited favor, and it is the gift that we receive through faith. Salvation is not something we can earn by our works but is a gift freely given by God. This grace not only saves us but sustains us in our walk with Christ, and it is the foundation of our hope for eternity.

The Last Ash: How does the gift of grace shape your view of salvation and your relationship with God?

The Final Sip: How can you live today in gratitude for God's grace, knowing that your salvation is secure in Him?

December 31

New Purpose and Possibilities

"But from everlasting to everlasting the Lord's love is with those who fear him, and his righteousness with their children's children." (Psalm 103:17, NIV)

While seasons and circumstances change, God's love remains constant—stretching from everlasting to everlasting. No matter what lies ahead, we can be confident in God's unchanging character and His promise to walk with us and our families through every season. With Him, each new year is filled with purpose and possibilities.

The Last Ash: How has God shown His faithfulness to you in the past year?

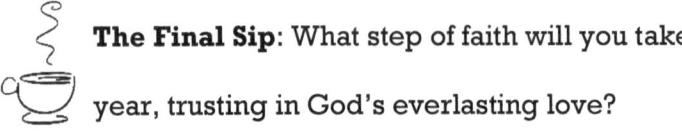

The Final Sip: What step of faith will you take in the new year, trusting in God's everlasting love?

To reiterate, men, you are not in this alone and remember always, it's not how you start, it's how you finish.

Please pray for us and consider partnering as we look to make disciples of all nations using these resources, tools, and social events.

To further enhance your walk with Christ and join our team and mission, consider leading a HOLY SMOKES chapter in your area.

To learn more, visit holysmokescoffee.org.